THE SNOWBALL EFFECT

By Randolph Mark Casey Snowball

The Snowball Effect

Randolph Mark Casey Snowball

ISBN 978-0-557-00271-9

PROLOGUE

Within these pages unfolds a story that almost everyone can identify with in some way, shape or form. The range of topics I discuss are vast and extremely humanistic: from our first love; to our first cigarette; to the first time we ever truthfully looked inside ourselves and abounded with the strength to admit that our evolving ideals might be wrong.

Each of us has a fascinating story behind the evolutionary process of our spiritual growth, but this is not a book about religion. It is a book about the many things we think about in coming of age, but for some reason rarely discuss with anyone but ourselves.

Let's face it; we live in a very untrusting society in terms of personal relationships. How often do we find someone with whom we genuinely feel comfortable or trust enough to tell the story of our life?

This is mine, from ages 5 to 19. Some of it is disturbing. Some of it is funny. Some of it is sad and some of it is just plain weird.

After writing this book, I came to realize, in so many ways, how truly desperate I am for direction and guidance and what a publicized cry for help this book really is.

You be the Judge.

I've spent days hitchhiking on desolate freeway on-ramps watching the sun go down. I've walked for miles on highways with no traffic in the burning 100-degree heat. No money, no food, no water. I've slept under freeway overpasses in Los Angeles where I've watched people get knifed; stumbled onto the decomposed bodies of dead junkies; and been offered money to let fags suck my dick, fuck 'em in the ass with hammer handles and pee on their back, while calling them a worthless faggot punk, for 40 bucks and a 12 pack; none of which I agreed to participate in, except the last, for which my answer to the proposition was, "I ain't drinking' yet?" What the hell? Huh? I've busted into crack houses, stuck a pistol in the dealer's mouth and demanded dope and money. I've had mother fuckers dive through my drivers side window for the ignition keys, got 'em in a headlock, started beatin 'em in the face, only to be drug out by my feet through the passenger side by another guy and then carjacked, and gotten away, keys, car, and all. I've been pulled over twice in one day by the LAPD with a pound of meth in the car and a 41 caliber in the console, and drove away both times. I've been in knife fights, bar fights, car chases and street fights. I've had my ass kicked, backed down, backed up, stood strong, stood weak, fought for what I thought was right, fought for what I knew was wrong. I've been possessive, obsessive, excessive, aggressive and I don't mind sayin' so. I've hitch hiked 13 miles a day every day for 6 months so I could work a 10-hour shift

at $4.25 an hour.

My father was just plain mean and actually quite violent. At times, I was terrified of him. He had an explosive temper and sometimes physically abused my Mom. I remember a fight that began when my father had misplaced his keys one morning and was late for work. He exploded a little more with each tick of the clock until finally concluding that my mother must have hidden them from him so he couldn't go to work...so that she wouldn't have to watch the kids. He broke her nose that day; the first of 3 times he would do so. After they separated it was just the three of us, my mom Becky, my sister Marie and me "little Markus Parkus" or little Marky. My sister was (is) a year older than me and very protective as I was a very passive little boy. My Mom didn't have a car so sometimes we did an awful lot of walking. I was so little I couldn't walk very fast and to this day I still remember both of them arguing, Mom saying "Marie slow down and wait for your brother". They would both stop and wait for me, frustrated. "Come on slow poke hurry up!" they would say. I would try to hurry as fast as my little legs would carry me. I can vividly recall wanting to catch up with them so I could feel secure again, but at the same time being afraid of catching up to within an arms length because I knew they were mad at me. Thanks dad! Fortunately for me, my Mom and sister loved me very much and by the time I would finally catch up, they would both be standing there saying "how cute", with a frustrated maternal ogle. The three of us managed to get our own little place on several different occasions. In one place in particular, my sister and I were suppose to be at school one day, but we skipped and figured we'd just swing all day at the apartment complex playground. I was swinging and sis was pushing...we were just having a good ole time until suddenly I hear sis scream "Its MOM!!" I was absolutely paralyzed in that swing when I saw Mom making a "B" line straight for 'little Mark'. Ya see, I was a *freezer* and Marie, well she was a *runner*, and when I say runner I mean she ran like an antelope straight out of "Mutual of Omaha's Wild Kingdom." It was later determined that she could go from zero to 60 in .3 seconds, but Mom was relentless and would always corner her. We got spotted by someone in the apartment complex, who then promptly went straight to Mom with something most assuredly to the effect of, "Didn't I just see Mark and Marie down at the swings?" I know for a fact what she said, "SAY WHAT"! Oh, we got our asses beat that day, but we weren't the only ones who got our asses beat by Becky C in those apartments.

One afternoon after coming home from school, I was alone, as Marie was often out either beating up some boy or playing Springbok when I noticed Mom at the top of the stairs. We lived in one of those apartments with the single narrow flight of stairs that led to two upstairs apartments, our door on the right and the door of the neighbor lady, whom apparently Mom felt wouldn't be needing her two front teeth or the use of her jaw anymore, on the left. I can vividly recall squeezing past her leg and into the apartment as she charged at the neighbor lady saying, "You fuckin oakie, bitch! Ya know what?" BOOM! SLAM! CRASH!! And that was it. She yelled, "and fuck you!" at the neighbor, slammed our door, and then turned to me and said, "Hi Marky, how was school, are you hungry? I'm making noodles." I said, "Can I help?" …She said, "No", and that it was almost done. Well the noodles were boiling and done so she reaches over to turn down the heat and the damn knob pops off. So here's Mom slapping at this 3-foot flame that's shooting out from where a knob use to be saying, "Marky go find the manager." So I run out and at the bottom of the stairs I run straight into Marie, BAM! She doesn't know about ole Mom up there slapping at that 3-foot flame, but she's a little curious about the ambulance rolling up. I forgot all about Mom beating up the neighbor lady. Right about then I see the manager coming to see what all the excitement is about. I run up to him yelling, "There's a fire, my Mom's on fire!" He looks up to see the reflection of firelight and Mom's shadow on the kitchen wall still slapping at the flames with a dishrag. So he goes running up the stairs and BAM! runs right into the toothless neighbor. The little stairwell is a bit crowded with Marie and me, the manager, two paramedics and the toothless oakie bitch. The manager is horrified at oakie bitch's face, she can't talk. We pushed through and I will never in my life forget the look on that woman's face when the manager shoved her aside and ran up to *our* place. My sister and I watched excitedly as he and my Mom swatted at the flame until finally the manager retrieved a screwdriver and managed to turn off the gas. I remember Mom explaining what had happened to the manager and him just laughing shaking his head. My Mom is always very animated in describing things. She is very down to earth, which makes her very hard to dislike. He said we'd better get outta there before the cops came, and they both agreed it'd be best if we moved. He didn't want to see her arrested for battery or lose her kids. She thanked him, told him to fix that stove, and we were gone.

3

The next place we moved into was an old project type of place. There were a lot of other kids, but I was kind of a loner. I really liked to explore and I did a lot of exploring with my best friend in the whole world, Uncle Bobby. The ages of my two Aunts and two Uncles ranged somewhere between 15 (Uncle Bobby), 14 (Aunt Julie), 16 (Uncle Ronnie), and 18 (Aunt Pamela); my Mom being the oldest at 20 something. My Uncle Bobby and I were tight, more like brothers. He used to take me roof jumping, where he'd hold my little legs and I would ride his shoulders with my arms wrapped around his forehead while he'd jump from project rooftop to project rooftop. I'd be on his shoulders giggling all wide-eyed and delirious, intoxicated you might say. We also went golf ball hunting. Grandpa would pay us money for collecting them. He'd polish 'em up and put 'em in egg cartons and then resell them to his golfer buddies. Now let me tell ya something about golf ball hunting. First of all it's private property and although it's already a huge golf course (everything's huge when you're small), they were always expanding. There was a lot of bulldozing going on. Well, guess where the golf balls were, that's right, in the underbrush. There was another danger lurking in that underbrush, jackrabbit nests. My Uncle Bobby would hoist me up over the fence, then he'd jump over and we would start crawling through the underbrush on our hands and knees and when it got really thick we would be on our bellies. That's where the rabbits were…in the thicket. I was on my belly the first time I got charged by a rabbit. I had no idea what it was and Bobby was out of my line of site at the time, but he was never far away. I was backed into a corner by a pissed off jackrabbit when Uncle Bobby came kicking' and swinging' through the underbrush like a human rototiller. Ole Bugs Bunny didn't want nothing' to do with him and made a quick retreat. "Damned Wabbits", he would say, and we would break into a silly giggle until we were both rolling' around in the weeds holding our bellies gasping for air. Uncle Bobby would explain the importance of not disturbing Bugs Bunny, mostly he said was because they could hurt me. The other reason he said was because they were there first and that we were the intruders. He was a joker. He would take me to what he referred to as "Wabbit World." We would crawl in on our bellies and he would be whispering like Elmer Fudd narrating a National Geographic's special on Bugs Bunny in his natural wabitat. (Whispering) "Here we are at Wabbit World Watching Waskly Wabbits". I'd giggle and he would say "shhhh", pointing at the biggest Wabbit saying, "look there's Bugs Bunny right there...lets get out of here!" Every once in a while we would get spotted by the bulldozer and when that happened I learned to instinctively hop on Bobby's shoulders and hold on for dear life as Bobby would play cat-n-mouse with the driver and narrowly escape by jumping the fence just as the driver bulldozed the thicket to the fence line.

My Uncle Bobby and I would take our hard earned golf balls to Grandpa where he'd inspect their quality and then hand some money to Uncle Bobby and say, "Pick me up a Chico Stick." He knew we'd be headed strait down to a tiny little neighborhood store two blocks away called "Harry's Market." Bobby would take me down there, carrying me on his shoulders like a little human trophy. To this day I have no idea how much money Grandpa gave Bobby, but by the time we left the store it seemed like we had bought at least two of every kind of candy on the shelf, plus ice cream and soda. We would head back home, and usually be joined by my sister Marie and some of the other kids in the neighborhood for the walk home. Sometimes Aunt Julie would see us and join the walk asking, "Where's my push-up", as that was her favorite kind of ice cream. Everyone got something, Uncle Bobby made sure of it. We would all walk back, our little group, laughing and giggling eating ice cream and candy.

I guess I should mention that the house I'm referring to is Grandma and Grandpa's house. My Mom didn't trust leaving her kids with just some babysitter, so sis and I pretty much grew up with our aunts and uncles at grannies. Plus there was always that fear that my Dad would show up at where ever we were living at the time. We didn't stay at the project apartments for very long.

I remember an occasion when good ole Uncle Ronnie was supposed to be keeping an eye on us. I came in from playing outside to find nobody home, so I got this idea that I was going to be a drummer. All I needed was a drum set and some sticks, so I made my way to the kitchen and promptly pulled out every pot and pan I could find. I used cookie sheets for cymbals; setting them on upside down Tupperware bowls. I wanted everyone in the neighborhood to see me be a drummer, so I set up my drum set right in the front doorway. I turned the pots upside down, grabbed myself some wooden spoons and began my first drum solo. It would prove to be the last drum solo I would ever perform. When Mom got home I could see in her eyes she was not impressed. The first things out of her mouth were, "Where is your Uncle Ronnie, where's your sister and what the hell do you think you are doing?" I had no answers for those questions. I was speechless and I made a "cry baby face" before any sound even came out of my mouth. I was quickly whisked into my room. I could hear Mom cursing Uncle Ronnie, putting all the pots and pans away and then standing in the doorway screaming at the top of her lungs, "Marieeee!" Pretty soon you would see this little girl bouncing like an antelope at top speed, you know, like Walt Disney's Bambi.

The next time Uncle Ronnie took off and left us to our own devices, Marie and I set out to explore this old garage or storage unit. We could see inside and it was filled almost to the roof with boxes. Well, we had to know what was in them and I don't know how... but we got in. We soon discovered that almost every box was filled to the top with matchbooks.

Wow! Matches, cool. We promptly filled our pockets and got out of there so we could commence to flickin'. We needed targets and we found just that in the dry ivy that had intertwined itself along the entire chain link fence line. Within that ivy were thousands of spiders sitting on their webs. Poor little bastards. I think it was only the third or fifth flick that it took to set the entire 100-foot fence line into a wall of flames. That day we were both *"freezers"* as we both watched in awe at what we'd done. When we heard the fire truck sirens, we didn't move…when the firemen rushed in with their hoses and proceeded to extinguish the flames, we didn't move…when the firemen pried the books of matches from our little hands, we didn't move. As a matter fact we were still frozen like wax figures staring at the charred remains of the fence line when Mom showed up. She simply took us both by our little hands and led us back to the apartment, while we both were still unable to take our eyes off of our handiwork. Mom was incredibly understanding about that day. She could see how freaked out we were and you didn't have to be a rocket scientist to see that we would never play with matches again…and we never did. Besides that, I think Mom beat Uncle Ronnie up for not keeping an eye on us.

4

After that we had to move into Grannies. All we could say was, "yaaaaay" Grannies! It was nine people in a 2-bedroom house. Pamela and Ronnie were hardly ever there. I remember my room, which I shared with Marie. Marie always fell asleep before me. I would lie there awake and listen to Mom, Granny, and Aunt Julie and sometimes even Uncle Bobby. They would all stay up late talking about little Marky and Marie. There was a night I fell asleep with a huge wad of bubble gum in my mouth and woke up with it in my hair. If I recall, the only reason I even got up was because I was sick and had a fever. I didn't even know about the ball of Bazooka in my hair until I got up and walked into the kitchen where Mom and Granny were up talking. "Hi Markus Parkus, what's wrong honey?" I was hugging Mom's leg, burning' up, when she noticed the wad of Bazooka Bubble gum in my hair. "What do you have in your hair? Oh my god, where in the world did you get all of that bubble gum" and before I could answer they both looked at each other and simultaneously said, "Bobby!" Uncle Bobby was asleep on the couch when Granny started yelling into his ear, "Bobby P, did you give little Marky all that bubble gum? Just look at that, look at his hair! Now how are we going to get all of that gum out?" By this time I was giggling. Still sick, but giggling, mostly because I was getting all that attention. When Uncle Bobby rolled over wearing his glow in the dark Dracula teeth and said "Why donta we trya peanuta butter blah, blah," everyone was giggling. We were all laughing when all at once we noticed Marie standing in the hallway with a scowl on her face, as if to say, "How dare all of us be giggling without her." Soon she joined the fun of running peanut butter through my hair. I would never go so far as to say Marie was ever jealous of me, it's just that anyone who'd have been watching from where Marie was standing, would have had the same longing for that love and levity. Nobody could watch our lives without longing to be a part of it, but it wasn't always "Little House on the Prairie." There were times Uncle Ronnie would tickle me until I couldn't breathe. He never knew when to quit, because I really couldn't breathe, so I'd start crying. There was also an occasion when Uncle Ronnie and Aunt Julie sat me in a chair in the corner of the kitchen and made me repeat after them, "Hallo weenie." They would say that word in a low demonic sounding voice and then tell me, "Say it!" I would mimic them and I guess it sounded real funny the way I did it because they just kept making me do it. What they didn't seem to realize is that the longer they did it the more demonic it began to sound to me. I finally got so scared I began to cry and say, "no" in that chilling little shrill only a little kid can do. Mom came charging in, "What are you guys doing to Marky? Leave him alone, you're scaring him!" They tried getting me to do it for Mom, but I was too scared by then. So she made them quit, and there was a phobia moment when Marie and I went to a neighborhood park to play. I spent most of the time on the swings, trying to swing as high as I could so I could jump off and fly through the air. Somehow Marie talked me into climbing to the top of the rocket slide. Now the rocket slide was a hollow rocket tube with a spiral staircase that went all the way up to the pointed cone and there was a steel platform where you'd wait your turn, climb through a hatch hole (simulated) and slide down. I got about as far as the platform, watched Marie slide down and then froze! There is no way in hell I was going down that slide. At first Marie tried talking me down. "Come on Mark!" she'd say sternly, but I would just start crying. She couldn't understand how I could jump off that swing and fly through the air so fearlessly, but then turn around and freeze up on a slide. She tried coming up and getting me, but I wouldn't let go of the rail. She finally just left me up there and went home. I sat up there and cried for what seemed like forever, but was probably only about 20 minutes. It was Uncle Bobby, of-course, who came and rescued me. He climbed the stairs slowly singing the theme song to "Mighty Mouse" complete with whooshing and shooshing sounds. By the time he reached me, I was already in a full blown giggle, and then he said in his best Mighty Mouse voice, "Hop on and hold on tight!" I did and we took the slide down together, over and over and over, until it started getting dark and was suppertime.

Ya know...I only ever saw Uncle Bobby get mad once. It was late, well past my bedtime anyway. I was supposed to be in bed, but when I heard the front door close, I ran out to look through the window in the door just in time to see Uncle Bobby pick up Aunt Julie's bicycle, raise it above his head and slam it back down into the ground as hard as he could…about 5 times. The thing looked like a ball of tin foil when he was done. I guess Aunt Julie should have taken her own bike instead of Bobby's (oops).

If there was one dude you never wanted to piss off it was Grandpa. Though I only ever saw this happen once, it was more than I needed to see. On a day when it was just Gramps and I, and everyone else was out playing, we were sitting in the kitchen eating graham crackers, (something Granny had forbidden him to do with us kids before dinner…we would always sneak them anyway)…when suddenly there was a knock at the door. We had one of those framed glass window doors. You know, the kind with the paned rectangles all the way to the bottom so that you could see the feet of whoever knocked. Well, I didn't have to see the feet to know who it was. I knew the knock. It was my Dad. Grandpa asked, "Who is it?" And when he heard, "Its Randy!" his eyes got as big as black checkers. He said, "Marky don't you open that door, I'll be right back" and then slipped out the back. I heard some commotion, and then it got quiet. Granny came home and asked me where Grandpa was. I was just about to answer her when Bobby and Julie came bursting through the door and said, "Mom, Mom, Dad's chasing Randy Casey around the block with a kitchen knife!" Right about then, we all heard the door to Randy's truck shut and then the engine start followed by old Grandpa yelling, "Get the hell out of here and don't come back, you son of a bitch!" Grandpa would have killed Randy that day, had he been able to catch him. Nobody was going to hurt his little girl or grandkids and then think he could just come knocking. That was the only time I saw Grandpa get mad.

My grandfather was a painter; he painted cars and girls together, though he hated driving. I remember going somewhere in a car with him once. It was, "Jesus, look at this idiot! Where do these people get their licenses?" and "Look at this dumbass, he's doing 35 in a 40. Go around... Go around! Watch it!! Watch it! (horns honking). Up yours asshole! Well if this guy would do the speed limit, I wouldn't have to tailgate him!" We were lucky to get home in one piece. But Grandpa was a very kind and gentle man when it came to his family. I just don't think he was very impressed with people in general.

Granny was funny. I had a thing about biting... she would be standing in the kitchen washing dishes and I would run up all of the sudden and bite her on the butt. She would chase me down and bite me back on the butt, of-course, I would cry, but that didn't stop me from doing it again. It was weird, it's like I would get this strange adrenaline rush just being near certain family members; my Mom, Granny and Marie. Sometimes I would just have to run up and bite them! The only time I can recall ever biting someone who wasn't family was one time in a supermarket. I was in the cart while Marie was pushing. Mom was on aisle 4, or somewhere, when we came upon a little black boy sitting in a cart. His Mama must have been on another aisle. Now this was all very disturbing to me because I had never seen a black person before. Marie said, "Look Marky, it's a little chocolate boy." Well...I guess I almost bit his finger off trying to get a taste. Some of the most memorable days while living at Grannies were the days when all of us kids; me, Marie, Aunt Julie, Aunt Pamela, Uncle Bobby, Mom, and sometimes even Uncle Ronnie would all sit captivated around the T.V. for an afternoon episode of Star Trek. It was like we were hypnotized. The only interruption would be when Bobby would go to the store for everyone. He would ask what everyone wanted and we would all say, "Shhhh!" He would be almost out the door when Pamela would say, "Bobby, Dr. Pepper." He would always come back in record speed, so not to miss any of the show, but he always brought back something for everyone, then there would be a lot of cellophane wrapper noise followed by, "Shhhh, quiet"...(how funny!) The other show we (mostly me and Marie) would watch fanatically was the Jackson 5. Marie and I would learn the songs by heart and sing along. It seems like the older and bigger I got, the closer Marie and I became. We would walk and sing together more and more. I guess you could say she taught me how to sing. She also taught me how to whistle, skip, run, jump and swing.

5

Let's talk about Marie while we're on the subject. Marie was tough, a lot tougher than me. She was very protective of me, but she has a mean streak too. On a day Mom was running a bath for me, I must have done something to piss her off (Marie), because she decided to go into the bathroom and turn the cold water off while leaving the hot water to fill up the tub. I went to get into the tub, stuck my right foot in and burnt it, 3rd degree style. I had to be rushed to the hospital and Mom had to tend to my foot for more than a month. I still have scars to this day. Of course I wasn't always a perfect little angel and I recall one occasion when Marie must have done something to piss me off. The only thing I really remember is smashing her in the head with a crystal owl that sat on the nightstand. I don't know why, but I do know that it was the meanest thing I ever did to her.

Eventually we moved out from Grandma's to a house in a place called Box Canyon. We shared the house with some friends of my Mom's. I don't remember very much about them, just that they were nice and there was a pretty girl who lived there who was pregnant and due in April. It was out in the boonies, as opposed to the inner city of Los Angeles. We slept in the loft that you reached from a ladder in the den. I think my Mom worked at a club called "Apple Annie's" at that time. I vaguely recall watching her lace up her red clodhopper knee high boots, getting ready for work a time or two. All three of us did a lot of singing together at that time. We would sing songs like, "Midnight Train to Georgia", "Don't Rock the Boat", "Me and Mrs. Jones"...Motown.

Oh yea! We would sing all the time. There was actually a door of sorts that opened upstairs in the loft. At night, there was a strange squeaking sound that came from behind that door, but you could only hear it late at night, when we were trying to sleep. I would be lying there and it would happen; squeak, squeak, squeak! I would whisper to Marie, "Did you hear that?" "Yea, I heard it too." "You guys be quiet and go to sleep!" Mom would say, but eventually she started hearing it too. "What the hell is that, do you guys hear that?" Well somehow, don't ask me how, Marie already knew what it was. She said, "It's a bat" and that's exactly what it was. Mom said, "What, how do you know Marie?" "Cause I seen it." "How?" "Just open that door." We all three got up, went over to where this little door was and opened it... and there it was flying sporadically, since apparently it wouldn't come home until we shut the door. So we did. Marie said as long as we left it alone, it would leave us alone, so we simply got use to the squeaking at night.

For me, the unfortunate thing about moving out of Grannies was that it meant I had to go stay with my Dad on some weekends. I hated that! I was so afraid of him that I would start bawling when he'd show up in his blue truck to pick me up. My Mom felt sorry for me, but I don't think there was a whole hell of a lot she could do about it. It was either that or Randy would make trouble. I think the only reason he would come and insist I go with him, was to show he still had a say in something. I know it wasn't so he could spend time with his boy, because all he would ever do is drop me off at one of his girlfriend's houses, where I would stay till it was time to go home. There was one girlfriend who had a boy of her own. He was much older than me, but whenever we would go there, the women's son (whose name I can't recall) and I would play in his room until it was time for my father and I to leave. On that last day we would ever visit, I was in the boy's room playing with rector robots, I heard some commotion, and I looked down the hall at the same moment my father's fist came across the kitchen table to flatten the woman's nose. I started crying instantly as I liked it there. I liked the woman (whose name I can't recall). I liked her son and he liked me. We were buddies. The kid could see I was scared to death of my father, yet he would take the time to go out of his way to make me feel like it was alright to relax and be a kid, even when my Dad was around. No one had ever been able to do that for me. It was a sense of security that I had never felt away from Marie, my Mom or Uncle Bobby. Most of the pain and fear I felt that day wasn't about having to leave with my Father, it was more about having to leave behind a sense of security that I was afraid I would never again be able to find. On top of that, I knew that once we left, I would never see those people again and ya know what, I never did! Later in life I would comprehend the rarity of coming in contact with people with the kind of heart and soul that that woman and her son were made of. Anyone who has experienced this kind of genuineness in a person knows exactly what I'm talking about.

I only ever met my Dad's side of the family once. They lived in Lancaster, California. I stayed there for 3 or 4 days and oh boy! I couldn't wait to leave. My Dad was gone the entire time while my Granny and Grandpa Casey watched me. Now from what I can remember, my Grandpa Casey was pretty cool. By the time I made it back home to Mom, he had filled my entire right shoe with silver dollars and fifty-cent pieces, but Granny was just a plain ole bitch...and that's all I'm going to say about them. Uncle Ronnie ended up stealing all my silver dollars anyway...fucker!

Things were going pretty well for us in Box Canyon. It was the holiday season, Christmas of 1972. Marie became incredibly fascinated with animals; horses, dogs, cats...it didn't really matter. We had a dog named Boozer. Boozer was our best friend. He went everywhere we went. There was a farmer up the hill from where we lived and we used to go up there and play along with a bunch of other kids from the neighborhood. Well, one day this farmer gave me, Marie and Boozer a ride home. Marie and I got out of the truck and when we started calling for Boozer... well, the old man just wouldn't let him come. I'll never forget Boozer's face when the farmer pulled away with him in the cab. The guy quite simply stole our dog. We never saw Boozer again, weird. After we lost Boozer, we didn't have a very high opinion of neighbors. We figured that if the farmer could steal our dog, then we could just go on ahead and steal everyone in the neighborhoods mail. The first couple of times we did it we hit pay dirt. It was Christmas ya know, people send $ during Christmas and pretty soon we had a lot of it ($), too much in fact. It wasn't long before Mom started finding the $, not to mention all of the envelopes addressed to every house in the neighborhood but ours. BUSTED! She made us take whatever money was left in the cards we hadn't touched yet back to the houses they were addressed to and then, of course, she beat our asses. We never did that again.

Now I mentioned earlier (with no great emphasis) something about my sister's fascination with animals. Her favorite animals were horses and right behind our house there was a stable full of horses. We use to watch a woman go to the stable and feed them everyday. Marie vowed to ride those horses one day. When the day finally came, she said to me, "Come on Mark! She just feeds the horses and drives away. Mom's at the store, so now is our chance!" We went over to the stable and Marie quickly rounded up an appaloosa for her to ride and a pony for me. She opened the gate and said, "Don't be scared Markus, it's going to be fun", and with that hoisted me up on the pony. She then followed suit and hopped up onto the appaloosa as if she'd been riding all of her life. We got out onto the road and things were going just dandy. You ever see that Walt Disney movie, "Ride a Wild Pony?" Well, that was us. Just a riding and grinning...clip, clop, clip, clop, clip, clop...and then Bam! I got bucked off. I almost landed on my head and somehow got my finger smashed. Now, I can't remember if Marie also got bucked off or if she just dismounted, but she was by my side lickity split to make sure I wasn't hurt real bad. Right about the time we noticed the horses running off, Mom pulls up on her way back from the store. "Marky? Marie"? Is that you? Oh my God! Are you kids all right? What the hell are you kids doing? Whose horses are those? Get in the car ya little horse thieves." We got home and Mom put some ice in a stainless steel bowl to try and make the swelling in my hand go down. I could tell she was a little amused, but wanted to make sure we were all right. After she was sure she knew whose horses they were, she let the people know and the horses were recovered.

Not long after that happened, Marie and I spent the night at a babysitter's house up the hill from our house. The babysitter was this old man and he would watch a bunch of kids from the neighborhood at one time, like 10 at a time. We snuck out in the morning while everyone else was still asleep and walked back home. When Mom saw us coming (as she was out front), she asked us what we thought we were doing and told us to get our little asses back up to the old man's house. We did, and upon our return we were, of course, asked where we had gone. We replied that we had gone home, but that Mom had instructed us to come back. The old man sharply replied with, "Oh no, if your Mom is home, then its time to go home!" We knocked on the door at home for the rest of the day until it started getting dark. It was cold and our hands hurt from knocking. Our faces were dirty and snotty; our cheeks were frozen from crying all day, and the darker it got, the more desperate and hysterical our cries became. I was only 5 and Marie only 6. As tough as she was, she knew we wouldn't make it in the cold and where the hell was Mom? We both began to panic. Finally, it was neighbors who lived some distance away, that heard the high shrill of us crying, "Mom, let us in!" They came and took us into their home. They wrapped us in blankets, gave us a big bowl of popcorn to share and sat us in front of their big console T.V. to watch the Rose Bowl parade. It seemed like we were there forever, at least long enough that we thought we were waiting for Mom to pick us up. We were exhausted and finally fell asleep. We were still asleep when the Los Angeles Police Department officers carried us out to their squad car. Still wrapped in blankets we were promptly driven to the nearest hospital, where we were quickly checked for lice, injuries and other such things. Still bewildered and half asleep, we didn't fuss. Besides, I think we both just assumed that Mom would be coming along to pick us up at some point, but it was ten years before I'd ever see her again.

6

The cops dropped us off at a foster home. We only stayed there for two days and it would prove to be the first of many over the next 3 years. At the place we were taken to next, we stayed for a while...at least long enough for me to learn how to ride a bike on my own and with no hands. Ya see I had been trying to master this for months. I guess you could say I had been practicing all my life and the day I was finally able to do it for the first time I wanted to be acknowledged...especially by Sis. The lady (whose name I can't recall) had made dinner...it was getting dark and it was time to come in, but she couldn't catch me. What I would do is ride around the block and every time I would pass by the front of the house, I would simply speed up so I could ride by, in a full-blown giggle and say, "Look, no hands! I can do it! Look at me!" I must have done this four times. She wasn't impressed and sent her husband out to try and catch me. I kept doing the same thing to him, until I heard my sister screaming at this woman, "I want to see my brother ride." Now remember, they're all sitting around the table waiting for me, the woman's son, her daughter and two other foster kids. Now I think it goes without saying that if you take a kid from Mom and don't even bother to offer the slightest explanation as to where Mom went, or what happened, what you'll end up with is a very pissed off kid and an overprotective sister. We both became quite volatile in the long run; it just started happening for Marie first. Well, I hear Marie and decide to come in.

Hubby couldn't have caught me if he tried, so as I'm rolling in I hear some more commotion and bang, crash, slam! Here comes that dinner through the front window. I'm talking the main course, glasses, and plates, you name it, Marie's chucking it through the glass. I was quickly whisked into the back bedroom, where I slept, and told to just stay in my room. As the commotion continued, I lay on the bottom bunk looking for something to destroy. You see, Marie was all I had left and I was all she had left, so it was instinctive to act out together. That way they would want us both to leave, when it came time to call the police and welfare. There would be none of this, "Well the little boy is fine, but Marie is uncontrollable, so she'll have to go but Mark can stay." So as a precaution I would always follow Marie's lead. Well, this time I didn't have to look far. As a matter of fact at the same time I was looking for something to destroy, my feet were already doing the job for me as I ripped through the entire under liner of the top bunk. It might not have been so bad if the bed hadn't only been two days old. When they came in to check on sweet little Marky and discovered the damage I'd done, the woman just started bawling and we were picked up by welfare that night. All it would have taken to avoid the whole thing was for them to come out with my sister, watch me ride and say, "Wow!" As important as this was to me, what was important to this woman was that I do what I was told, when I was told to do it.

It really doesn't do any good now to speculate as to exactly what impact a little acknowledgement could have had on the future development of my self-esteem, but I can tell you this, the events of that day made enough of an impression to make me want to break up as I reflect upon it now, 32 years later. In light of what I was going through, I would say I was, or I should say "we", were doing pretty well at just being kids...considering there had *never* at any time been the slightest attempt to explain to us what had happened to our Mom. We were left to draw our own conclusions. Marie refused to believe that Mom had abandoned us, and fought every step of the way. Me, I was still sort of trying to figure out the social psychology of the world and myself. So I was a little (a lot) more cooperative, but that would change as I experienced more of the same kinds of insensitivities. But not yet!

We bopped in and out of several short-term foster homes until finally ending up with the "B" family. Now, the "B" family was a white family that consisted of Kathy and Jerry B. They also had a son and a daughter (whose names I can't recall). They lived in a trailer at the top of a hill in a trailer park with literally hundreds of trailers in it. Jerry was a police officer with the LAPD and a complete arrogant asshole. Kathy was a housewife and a physically abusive bitch. Nice package! This was a rough neighborhood. I got my ass kicked more times than I can remember, and not only by kids in the neighborhood, but sometimes by Kathy. Her favorite form of discipline was to slap us both in the face until our noses bled in an attempt to force us into admitting to wrong doings that she knew damned well were perpetrated by her own children. Oh yeah, she was a real piece of work. Needless to say we spent most of our days playing outside for as long as we could, but because of the neighborhood, that wasn't always a safe bet. Almost all of the experiences and memories I have of this place are vivid, as if they were yesterday. One memory in particular occurred on a hot late summer afternoon in 1973. I was six and riding my bike by myself through the trailer park at the bottom of the hill. Now the geography of this hill is such that if you were to head up it and arrived at the halfway point, there was a driveway that led off to the left and went down a ledge in the hill for about 60 yards. At the end of the driveway was a trailer. It was quiet in the neighborhood, and it seemed like I was the only kid still out on his bike when suddenly I began to hear a faint rumbling in the distance. I had never heard this kind of sound before in my life. I knew it wasn't an earthquake. I didn't know what the hell it was, but I did know one thing, it was getting incredibly loud and heading straight for me. I was just beginning to feel the flesh on my bones begin to vibrate when I noticed, coming around the corner, about 50 Hells Angels entering the trailer park. From where I was sitting on my Schwinn, it looked like they were coming to talk to me, but come on, I'm only 6. It just seemed like every last one of them made a point to get just to the spot where I was frozen on my bike and then suddenly turn left in the direction of the hill, but not go up it. They all parked just at the bottom of the hill and began to simultaneously *rev* their choppers until the sound was deafening and then all at the same time, they stopped. A window at the back of the trailer on the ledge slides open and a man with scraggly hair and a beard pops his head out and starts waiving a very large very shiny handgun while yelling something. As I think of it now, it reminds me of hijacker footage where the guy sticks his head out of an airliner and says, "I'll kill them! I'll kill them all!" These guys had a little conversation and then, just as suddenly as they came, they started up and were gone. As soon as I couldn't hear the rumble of their Harley's anymore, I got on my "Hog" and rode up to the top of the hill and home. I never spoke of what I saw that day to anyone, not because of fear, but because I would never have known where to start and at that age I didn't have the vocabulary to put it into words.

Every once in a while I liked to see how fast I could get going down that hill. I wanted to try it with no hands and just coast all the way down, but I was unable to ride my bike with no hands for any great distance and certainly not down a long steep hill. However on Marie's bike I had much better control and balance, so on the day I decided to try it, I stole her bike for the stunt. Besides her bike was a cruiser. It had a Banana seat with the full-blown Monkey style handle bars. A kid could coast and cruise, hands free, on this bike for a mile and that's just what I was doing, at I'd say oh about 30 mph when I hit those brand new speed bumps at the bottom of the hill. You see, we lived at the top of that hill and I hadn't been down it in a day or two so I had no idea that the highway district, in an attempt to slow traffic for children out of the goodness of their heart, had (within that day or two) just put in two of the hugest speed bumps ever recorded by the California Highway District. I hit the first bump; the bike takes one hop, the front wheel turns hard to the right, comes straight back down onto the second bump...as a result ejecting me onto the fresh soft asphalt, where I slide for a good ten yards, on my face, head, neck, breast, and chest area. The next thing I knew I was sprawled out on a lawn chair, surrounded by about ten kids from the neighborhood, including my sister Marie, wincing from the sting of Mercurochrome being dabbed on my wounds. It must have been a sight; me lying there stained with red antiseptic and ten kids hovering over me blowing. "Funny!" The relationship between the B family and my sister and I was a bad one. There was always an underlying tension, but I would have to say that the main reason why my memories of this place were so vivid was because it was the home at which my sister and I would become separated. It was as simple as getting into a car with a social worker and never going back, without explanation of course.

I was taken to the home of a single white woman, no children, very attractive, very caring and soft-spoken. I really liked her and we got along extremely well. She seemed to understand me and the reasons for my untrusting and leery disposition. She was very accommodating to these sensitivities in me and, although I cannot recall her name, I will never forget her. Unfortunately, I would only stay in her custody for what seemed like about a month. By this time I was, to say the least, a bit apprehensive about getting into that standard issue county vehicle and they must have known I would be, because what used to be a visit from one social worker was, for some reason, a visit from two that day. I was forced kicking and screaming into the car. The drive was long, dull and loathing the whole way. I hated these social workers and saw no choice but to instinctively protect myself from what I had come to know as the enemy, Love! It just seemed to me that every time I would go to a new home, establish the foundation for a new relationship, begin to relax and let my guard down, then "BAM!" - time to go. As a result it became an impossible to believe that anyone who claimed to "love me" was actually sincere or genuine, thus making my primary objective, "hurt them before they hurt me!" My mission was to ensure that no one could possibly consider the idea of loving a rotten little bastard. Who would want to love a kid who throws chairs at you, curses you with every name in the book, was disruptive, uncooperative and noncompliant. It was my goal to become more trouble than I was worth and why not? It made more sense than to allow myself to continue being deceived, betrayed and then abandoned. Besides I had plenty of frustrated confusion to fuel it.

7

The next place I was dumped off at was an orphanage called Hathaway Home for Children. There were literally hundreds of children there, ranging between the ages of four and eighteen. This place would be my home for the next two and one-half years. Located in the hills east of the San Fernando Valley near an area called "Big Tujunga", there were five separate houses surrounding a large circular plot of grass. Three of the houses were for boys; two were for girls. Each house was split down the middle with one half for young kids and the other for older kids. Each side had it's own front dayroom with couches and TV. There was a center room with accommodations for staff, basically a large sleeping quarters. The kitchen and dining area was also located in the center of the divide. Each age group sat down for dinner at different times, as the dining area could only accommodate seating for one side at a time. One group would simply eat an hour before the other group. The bedrooms for kids were located in the far corner of each side of the house. If you were a new kid, you got your own room until you started to make friends, play well with others, gradually become more familiar with the new environment, and until you became comfortable enough to share a room with whomever you happen to make friends with. Pretty slick actually, because they didn't require a new kid to attend school until the foundations for new relationships with new friends had long been established. This made for a very comfortable introduction into the academic environment of school. It's a lot easier to be the "newby" in a classroom if the only new person left to meet is your teacher.

Hathaway Home for Children was actually pretty cool. I made lots of new friends and I can't think of a staff member I didn't like. My favorites were a man named Mark, who was from England and talked with a very heavy English accent; a woman named Beverly, a woman named Melody, another woman named Lou, the school bus driver Shirley, and the therapist Mark. English Mark was really very cool. He was the one who helped me start my Beatles record collection. He took all of us little kids on field trips. Hathaway was a completely self-contained orphanage with their own pool, a gymnasium, a pre-school and kindergarten, and even their own stable with horses for us kids to ride. English Mark took us horseback riding quite often. We would go in groups of 8 to 10 and usually ride until we found a peaceful place to dismount. Then we would do a little exploring or Mark would read to us while we all sat in a big circle and listened. This guy was smart and had incredible patience. The things he would read to us were extremely well selected and designed specifically to provide psychological stimulation for an audience of children ranging between the ages of 5 to 10. Whenever Mark would read to us, he would read the stories like an animated narrator from Walt Disney. I'll never forget one day in particular, we had been out riding and were just headed back when we were all completely overwhelmed by the unmistakable smell of straight up shit! We all start looking around for the source, and though nobody has said anything, we're all clippety-clopping along wearing that "just-about-to-blow-chunks-expression" on our faces. Suddenly I notice this "Sloppy-Joe" looking substance sliding down a pant leg of the kid in front of me. What's really fucked up is that the kid's name is Colin. Now Colin was a "*shitter*" and that's all there was to it. He had absolutely no bowel control. I don't know if someone named him Colin for a joke or what, but he sure lived up to it.

We all had our problems and mine was a recurring nightmare I use to have where I would be running from an unknown and unseen being while completely surrounded by huge fiery flames. I would be sprinting, literally running for my life, constantly looking behind me and then awaken crying hysterically. It would take most of the night to get me to stop. Beverly would carry me to the bed in the staff's sleeping quarters and hold me till I fell back to sleep, if I did. If I didn't, I would usually spend the rest of the day with Melody. Melody was very attractive and I had a crush on her. Melody and I would sit on the couch and watch Looney Toons together. I would usually fall asleep with my head in her lap and leave a pool of drool on her crotch. She didn't seem to mind.

One of the older kids who played guitar noticed that I had an extreme fascination with music. I sang Beatles songs 24 hrs a day, 7 days a week. The only non-Beatles song that I ran into the ground was a song called "Guitar Man." As a matter of fact I played it so often that one of the older kids threw my 45 out the window and down a 300-foot embankment. I was crushed, but I got over it. Melody and English Mark use to sneak me up to the gym so I could play my Beatles albums. This was the only place I could play full sized albums. Sometimes we would sit in the coach's office listening to those albums for hours. Fun stuff! Lou was pretty cool too. She was good with kids. She took a trip to Africa once and when she came back to work, she had brought all of us kids souvenirs. She gave me a necklace that had some kind of a pit on it. It was supposed to bring me luck. She got pissed at me once for sticking my hands in her front pockets. She said it was inappropriate! I'm seven now. Is that the age at which the line is drawn between sexual suggestion and playful child innocence or just the first time I got my hand slapped?

Shirley... how does one begin to describe Shirley? Shirley was the bus driver for the on-site school. She was quite a character, very charismatic, very personable, a kind of a likeable scatterbrain. Shirley had a bad habit of losing things. One day she had somehow lost her bag lunch. I found it. Another day she lost her lunch money. I found it blowing in the wind on the side of a hill. "$5.00"... you would have thought I hit the lottery. I was so excited I was jumping around like a pogo stick repeating over and over, "Five dollars! I found five dollars! Five whole dollars." I showed English Mark and he said we had to post a message on the Community Bulletin Board and if no one claimed it, it would be mine. Shirley claimed it and gave me fifty cents as a reward...bitch! Likable kooky bitch. Somebody had to decide, do we let the kid just keep it or claim it? I wonder if it was she?

Mark, the house psychologist, was an interesting character. He was good looking, soft-spoken, with wavy brown hair and a beard. He usually came in around lunchtime and on his way to his office would stop at the table where all of us little kids were eating. He'd pick up an apple and twist it in half. We'd all yell, "Wow!" and he would go into his office. I had one hour a week with him and all I would ever do was play with Lego's. I'm sure he would ask me questions and we would talk, but I have no recollection of what our discussions were about. There was an occasion when Mark let me stack Lego's as high as I could. I asked if I could leave it standing until our next session and he had no problem with that. When I walked into his office the following week, I was amazed to see my tower still standing.

Another year had gone by. It was 1975 and I was eight and getting more courageous. Myself and four or five of the other kids my age started sneaking into the nearby woods, hiking and exploring. One day we all were hiking and discovered a concrete gutter that had been overgrown with weeds. It went down the hillside for about 100 feet and was at a vertical down slope. Somebody came up with the idea of sliding down it on trashcan lids. What a hoot! We would set the metal trashcan lids at the top, take a running start and then jump on the lid and slide like a freak all the way down. Yeeeee Haw! What made it especially cool was that the aluminum lids would shoot these amber sparks all the way down, but we got busted when they came looking for us. It's unfortunate that although the environment at Hathaway was positive in most every way there were still two questions that ruled my life every single minute...and every single day... that had gone completely ignored and unanswered. What happened to Mom and what happened to my sister, Marie? So, in my mind, until these questions were at lcast answered, there would be no happy ending.

8

Shortly after turning eight, I began to receive visits from a woman whom I had met on an outing. Every Saturday about fifteen of us would get on a bus and be driven to where we would meet with people interested in potentially adopting. We would spend the day with them, getting to know them, feeling them out. This was sort of a pre-adoption party, but these potential adoptive parents were serious. They may have had their eye on a specific child for quite sometime before the visits began. Waiting, watching, preparing. This woman's name was Dorothy, and if that necklace I got from Lou was meant to bring me luck, then it must have worked because the day I met Dorothy would prove to be the luckiest day of my life. Now I don't recall a lot of detail about our visits before the adoption, but I do remember our first meeting, the time I peed my pants. It was a picnic, or actually more of a watermelon feed, in my case. I ate so much of it I couldn't make it to the bathroom. Funny! Not to me. We were at a large house with a pool and Dorothy was a chaperone on the bus. I expected to see my sister Marie there and was so disappointed that I clung to Dorothy and cried all the way home.

Near the end of my stay at Hathaway, there was a huge fire burning in the hills of Big Tujunga Canyon. The big Tujunga fire was headed straight for Hathaway and we all had to be evacuated. We were loaded into vans and buses and driven to a place called Hansen Dam. We were to stay there, camped, until further notice or until it was safe. I stayed there for two days, but then was located by Dorothy and her family after learning of the evacuation and becoming concerned for my welfare. I stayed with them until authorities gave the okay for everyone to return to Hathaway. Upon my return I was surprised to see that everything was okay, except that the trees and grass had been burnt. Life went on at Hathaway Home for Children.

The older kid who had noticed my interest in music, decided to give me a guitar. He spent weeks refinishing it and when it was finally done, he gave it to me. I think I had it a total of two weeks, if even that, then one day something or somebody pissed me off and I smashed it into a million pieces. This action would become one of my trademarks.

After the separation from my sister Marie, I no longer had anyone to stick up for me. I didn't trust anyone but I had to find something that I could love and that I could trust wouldn't and couldn't betray, deceive or abandon me. I found those comforts in my stuffed dog and my Ronald McDonald doll, both of which I ended up ripping to shreds. The only reason I mention this now is because I think it's important to note that up to that point of my life my unwillingness to open up and trust people, ultimately led to the manifestation of my love and trust into inanimate objects, my stuffed animals. As I began to get older and mature, this manifestation broke down, of course, and when it did, I destroyed that manifestations memory in a confused desperate rage. I believed I could trust them, I believed I could love them and so when that became insufficient and unrealistic with maturity, my panic led to the frustrated and confused rage that destroyed them. I felt life, God, my sister, my Mom and all those people who claimed to care about me, had let me down and I didn't know what to do.

Finally the day came when I was to leave Hathaway and the adoption process was complete and finalized. I was ready. The Snowball family consisted of 2 new brothers and a sister, as well as Dorothy's husband, Ronald. The names of the children were as follows; Daniel Jay (11 months younger), Richard Jay (4 years older) and Melissa Robyn (3 years younger). Dan and Melissa were both adopted as babies, Rick was 10 years old at the time of his adoption and I was 8 ½ when I left Hathaway. I remember the evening Ron, Rick, and Dan came to pick me up. I vividly recall Ron flirting with the receptionist on the way out the door of the Administration building at Hathaway. We walked out to his little blue Ford Courier; I hopped in the back with Dan and Rick and away we went. Once we got out onto the highway, I started looking Rick over and when he noticed, he flipped me off. I just smiled and turned to my new little brother, Dan, and asked if he was allowed to get away with that all the time. I was curious to know what I was going to be able to get away with and how soon. Dan's reply was that he was always like that, and he was. The Snowball household more than made up for the stuffed animals. Their extensive list of pets spoke for itself, 15 cats, 4 dogs, 2 peacocks, some bunnies and two horses, and plenty of love.

Since Rick pretty much always acted like a dickhead and Dan was closer to my age, it was Dan and I who lived all of the adventures. Dan was a very cool, mellow, easy-going kid. We got along excellently. We had our moments, but usually only when I was being a bully or just plain mean, which would also become another one of my trademarks, but not so much now as later on in the book. I started school at Sulphur Springs Elementary. We would catch the bus early in the morning at a bus stop located at the end of our street, Silver Star Lane. It was then that something very strange occurred. For two weeks when I first started catching the bus, I would be standing in the cold with Dan, along with various other kids from the neighborhood, when two ravens would swoop down and land at my feet and begin to caw frantically. If I tried to walk away they would follow me... they would walk right along with me. I even walked all the way back up the street to the house to show Dorothy. She didn't know what to make of it, but they would only walk with me and constantly cawed. They would only approach me at the bus stop in the morning. It happened for two weeks like clockwork and then "poof" they were gone. Weird.

9

I made new friends in the neighborhood and even some enemies. One day in particular I had been playing in the back yard with my new brother Dan, a kid named Joey, and a new kid in the neighborhood named Mike. We were in the back yard at our house when I noticed this Mike kid was being a bully to my new little brother Dan. By now I'm nine and I'm pretty sure I can take care of this so I warn the kid and tell him that if he keeps picking on my brother I would take him out into the street and kick his ass. He says, "I'd like to see you try." So.... we walk out into the street and right at the time he turns around to say come on, I jump kick him in the chest and he's on his ass. He gets up and starts running down the street as Dan and I chase him. Apparently, Joey chooses Mike's side so we chase both of them all the way to the bottom of the street. Mike's house was the last house on the block and when he got there he was met at the door by his father who then took off his belt and handed it to Mike who then chased Dan and I back to our house. We barely made it inside when they started (Joey and Mike) bombarding our house with dirt clods. At first we didn't know what to do and then it hit me. I said, "Hey... doesn't Rick have some wrist rockets in his room?" Dan says, "Yea, but it's locked." I said, "Let's go!" We busted into his room and quickly retrieved his wrist rockets. We didn't know what we were going to use for ammo at first but then it hit me. I looked at Dan and said, "We got any carrots?" We both look at each other, "Yeah." We

5

pulled them out of the fridge and start chopping 'em up. I find the biggest fattest one and chop it off at the butt. We've got a sliding glass door at the front of the house, just to the side of the front door. I look at Dan and say, "Watch this." I slide the door open about ¼ of the way...I put the carrot butt in the wrist rocket and pulled that fucker back as far as I could. You ever see one of those 3-D movies and the way they show objects just kind of float and sail through the air at a super high velocity? Well, that's exactly what this carrot butt looked like as it went straight down Mike's throat at about 60 or 70 MPH. We both (Dan and I) simultaneously turned to each other and howled, "Yea!" What a shot! A couple days later Dan and I ran into Joey and Mike while out hiking in some near by hills. Mike was very apologetic, why not? The poor kid had blue purple mangled lips and no front teeth. We shook hands and there were no hard feelings, but after that ole Mike was in no hurry to hang out with us and I'd be willing to bet he isn't too fond of carrots to this day.

There was a family right across the street from us and we were at *all out war* with the kids there; from stink bombs, to dirt clod fights, to bottle rocket wars, to wrist rocket wars... you name it. There were four of them, but only two were really rotten bastards. Their names were Orlando and Garth. They were both older than Dan or I, Garth being the younger of the two. One day we were having some kind of war with Garth. An egg war, I think. Well I must have run out of ammo or something because I ended up getting chased up a tree. Now I don't know about you, but there's only one thing to do when someone is climbing up after you in a tree, pee on the fucker. At first Garth wasn't sure what that moisture was until I started hitting him with a nice steady stream. Then it was, "What the? Is that? EWWW! It's pee!" I never saw a kid climb back down a tree and run home so fast in my life.

At about the time I was nine, Dorothy and Ron told me that my sister Marie had been located and would be coming to visit. You can't imagine what this meant to me. I was overwhelmed with joy! A widow had adopted Marie by the name of Vivian T. Vivian had a home in Acton, California, which ironically was relatively close to Canyon Country where we lived. Marie's visit took the weight of the world off of my shoulders, but there was something uneasy in her disposition. At the time I just attributed it to what had happened to us and it wasn't until years later that I found out what it was...which I'll talk about later in the book. In addition to visits from Marie, I was allowed to visit Marie. Two visits I recall where I was allowed to stay the weekend and it was great. They had four ponies and a lot of other pets, and we had the greatest time riding them and spending time together... relishing the reunion we never thought would happen. When it was time to go home, you know I didn't want to go. Marie was strong and assured me that we would not lose contact and would someday even find Mom. She said if I ever wanted to send a message to blink my eyes as fast as I could and just think of her and the message would be sent. We both agreed to this pact and I went home. One other thing, Marie reassured me that I had a good family and they loved me and I would be all right. Without that reassurance coming from her I'd have had to be dragged to the car kicking and screaming. She knew what she was talking about, as I would only become closer to the Snowball family.

Shortly after my adoption it came time to meet Dorothy's parents. My new grandparents were Jack and Belle. I'll never forget the look my new grandmother gave me the first time she laid eyes on me. As I describe it now I have to say it was the look of a woman who with her eyes said, "This is my new grandson to whom I am totally and completely committed to love as my own blood without condition." The love I would come to know from both of my new grandparents was a kind of doting love I had never known. They would often take all four of us to Toys R Us and grandpa would say, "Get whatever you want", and we did. I soon began to feel uncomfortable with so much love and began to become suspicious when it became obvious that no relocation was in sight. Being relocated was something to which I had become accustomed, and quite frankly the thought of my presence not becoming tiresome to this new family in my life was something I hadn't considered or even fathomed. I was getting comfortable. There was nothing I could do about it and it was pissing me off in a huge way. How dare these people love me! Not only did an increased comfort zone mean a more faded memory of my Mom, which I had vowed to disallow, but the circumstances of my previous situations had inadvertently caused me to convince myself that this love was not genuine and if it really were like they were trying so hard to make me believe, then I felt I had every right to test it. The trouble is that by having no conscious recollection of what being "genuinely loved" consisted of meant I had no way of knowing where the line between testing that love and accepting it started and stopped. But the more I was loved, the more distrusting and disruptive I became. Sort of a blurry confused anger began to creep up into my disposition and my way of testing could be downright cruel.

A good example is the day Dorothy was driving from school to school picking us up. Dan and I were in the back seat and something (I don't know what) pissed me off and I start kicking Dan in the face with my waffle stompers. Melissa started screaming in that high hysterical shrill she was so well known for. Dorothy slams on the brakes and yells; "Randy!!!" pulls to the side of the road and as soon as she stops I jump out and start running. Dorothy chases after me and after some discussion talks me back into the car. Ron tried to discipline me at times, but I was a very difficult child to discipline...and I showed him very little, if any, respect as a father figure. The relationship between Dorothy and Ron was rocky at times and would eventually wind up in divorce. It would be irresponsible if I were to even begin to speculate that I knew what caused this, except to say that I know

Ron drank and that my disruptive behavior had to have added some degree of strain to an already full plate. The details only Dorothy and Ron would know and that's their business.

On a short note that should have been explained much earlier on in this book, it should be known that my Mother and Father could never agree on my first name. On my Mom's side of the family my name was "Mark", but my Father wanted me to be a junior, so on my Dad's side I was "Randy." When I was adopted, Dorothy and Ron took my birth name of Randolph Mark Casey and added Snowball to the end, thus forever making me Randolph Mark Casey Snowball.

10

In the summer of 1977, a decision was made by Dorothy and Ron that absolutely devastated any chance of remaining near my sister Marie, and as far as I was concerned any possibility of ever seeing my natural Mother again. We were to move to Boise, Idaho. I used to lie awake in bed at night recalling all of the faces of women I had seen that day and ask myself, "Was this one my Mom? Was it the clerk in the store? What would I say if I saw her? Would I know if I had seen her? Was the picture of her in my mind really what she looked like?" The picture I had was faceless. The list of questions goes on, but every hope I might have had of ever seeing her again was destroyed the day I was informed of our move. I also use to think that the sound of my heartbeat when I laid my head on a pillow at night was actually the sound of my father's footsteps walking down a long corridor on his way to work, briefcase in hand. Now I knew I would be moving far enough away to not have to hear that anymore, the only bright side I could find about the move.

It took several months of preparation before the move. Selling the horses, deciding which animals would come along, the packing, the finding a home in Boise and a host of other responsibilities that as a ten year old, I couldn't even fathom. In any case, the fuse to my deteriorating attitude had already been lit. There was a short time before the move when Dorothy and Ron had separated. Ron had a little apartment with a Vietnam helicopter pilot. I know this because once on a weekend visit I became bored of watching "F-Troop", "Bonanza" and "Wild Wild West". Ron was passed out as usual so I started snooping around. I hit pay dirt when I found his roomies ammo stash. I loaded up my pockets and waited for Ron to wake up and take me home. God knows what my intentions were. It was just neat having bullets. It's a damn good thing there were no guns to be found, who knows what I would have done. When Ron drove me back to the house, it was late so I went to bed immediately. It must have only been about an hour later when I heard Ron's Ford Courier pull back into the driveway and then "Where is he?" "He's in bed." "That kid's going to get me killed." I was scared, but I couldn't help but giggle to myself a little when I heard him say that, because to tell you the truth I didn't like the guy much. I kind of gloated at the idea of my being responsible for him being afraid for his life. My bedroom door came open, the light flicked on and Dorothy said, "Just give me what you took from the apartment and that'll be the end of it, you can go back to bed." It sounded reasonable to me, so I did and that was that. So much for weekend visits with Ron. They only got back together when Dorothy agreed to move to Idaho. It finally came time to move and the plan was that Ron, Melissa and I would drive up ahead of Dorothy, Rick and Dan. So Ron put a camper on his Ford Courier, we packed it full of clothes, us kids, two dogs and two cats, and hit the road. On the way through Northern Nevada, we hit some serious snow and some wind gusts that almost blew us over a couple of times.   We only made it as far as Carson City, blew the motor and had to stay in the camper for a couple of days while Ron talked with Dorothy on the phone trying to decide what to do, replace the motor or buy a new truck. It was finally decided that Grandpa Jay (Ron's father), who lived in Boise, would come rescue us and drive us the rest of the way to Boise. Dorothy, Dan and Rick, two dogs and two cats caught up with us a couple of weeks later. They arrived the same day as the Global Movers truck.

11

9027 Woodside Court in Boise was truly a great house. We would soon settle into a neighborhood that would prove to be the classic residential accommodation for four young kids to grow up in. The first order of business was room assignment. Now this was a four thousand square foot house; the downstairs basement had two dens, three bedrooms, a bathroom and laundry room. The two bedrooms that would be Dan's and mine weren't quite finished, some drywall and carpeting still had to be completed. One of the dens came with a pool table, a wood stove and was carpeted, our own billiards room. The other den, at the opposite end of the basement, was just a big empty room with a piano and brand new linoleum. This is the room Dan and I would share until our rooms were done. One of the first things we discovered about what we quickly dubbed "the playroom" was that we could get a running start from the carpeted hallway and then slide all the way across the room into the wall. It was fun. Especially after we figured out how furniture polish made it real slippery. Pretty soon we had the family dogs running and sliding with us. These were truly lovable dogs, Valentine and Poppy. They would do anything with us. I became close to Valentine immediately after my adoption and I loved that dog to death, "literally." One of the great things about the "playroom" was that it was big enough so that we could set-up any kind of racetrack we wanted. We were into Hot Wheels. We (Dan and I) also had an extensive Lego collection, Lincoln logs and every Fisher Price town on the market, complete with people and cars. We would have make-believe races and go on make-believe dates, driving my TRANS AM Hot wheel. I'd be Gene Simmons and Dan would be Peter Chriss, band members from our favorite rock band, "KISS." But soon our bedrooms would be finished and we'd have our own rooms. When asked what kind of carpeting I wanted in my room I decided on a very loud pattern of all the classic board games; Backgammon, Checkers, Chess. It was wild looking.

We quickly made friends with kids in the neighborhood, played hide and seek, went exploring on our bikes. In the meantime I was enrolled into Eastside Elementary. It didn't take long to figure out that I had a serious problem with authority. My biggest problem was with those teachers that had that "how dare you challenge my authority" attitude. The ones whose faces would turn red, appalled at the slightest hint of non- compliance, would become my main targets for rebellion. I discovered, long before school, that a few well placed "fuck you's" or "make me's" is all it would take to get out of class for the rest of the day. I wasn't afraid of Dorothy or Ron because as far as I was concerned, discipline only served to prove my point that nobody really loved me and those who tried, in my eyes were only trying to set me up for betrayal once I let my guard down. So it became my mission to stay on the attack through shock value.

Sometimes, I went so far overboard that I even scared myself. For example the day Rick and three of his high school buddies came home from school for lunch. I was suspended from school, as usual, and listening to my Pink Floyd "Wish You Were Here" album in the billiard room of the basement. Now anyone who has sat down and listened to the first song on side one of this album "Shine on You Crazy Diamond" knows how meditative and sedative it is. So here I am, minding my own business and, for some unknown reason, one of Rick's buddies by the name of Mitch P. decides he's going to start poking at me...not recommended! This guy starts poking and prodding and pushing my buttons until finally I turn on him and say, "You know what mother fucker? You keep fucking with me and I'm going to fuck you up!" Unfortunately for him... he didn't take me seriously and kept fucking with me. When I was finally at the end of my rope, I ran upstairs opened the knife drawer, grabbed two ten inch carving knives, ran back downstairs, handed one of the knives to Mitch, kept one for myself, yelled, "Come on!" I went "WAK", hacking the back of his left hand and his pinky almost completely off. They all stood back in shock and disbelief and said "Holy Shit" and I have to admit I was pretty shocked at what I had done. They rushed him off to the hospital and I never heard another thing about it.

As shocked as I may have been, my behavior just became worse and worse. I would do things at home like burst into Dan's room while he was napping and call him "drooler boy" while I socked him on the arms and legs

56

"Ow, ow fucker", he would say while trying to block my hits. But I loved Dan and I really missed sharing a room with him. If I wasn't trying to bully Dan, I was terrorizing Melissa, and that was easy. All I had to do was poke at her or call her a name or two and she would start crying hysterically. Sometimes, I would be picking on both of them and they would call Dorothy at work. It was my way of including Dorothy in the "terror of the day" by letting them dial her work number and when she would answer I would pick up a phone in another part of the house and simultaneously make cry baby sounds while they complained about being picked on..."waa, waaa." Dorothy would be fuming and yelling into the phone at me, "GODDAMNIT RANDY, STOP IT!" STOP IT...LEAVE THEM ALONE!" I don't know how the woman put up with it, God bless her heart because she has plenty of it.

Before the knife incident with his friend, Rick and I never really hung out. His being four years older made a difference, and the fact that he grew to be 6'4 in height made him an unlikely target to bully. Besides, he never really bothered me and I didn't bother him...but it's amazing the kind of notoriety you get after you "hack" one of your older brother's friends. The first thing that happened was that suddenly one day out of the blue, Rick takes me into the back yard and says, "Dude, if you show me how to inhale (cigarettes), I'll let you hang out with me and my friends." You see, Rick knew I had been smoking since before we moved from California but, up to this point, Rick had always been a jock into basketball, track...that sort of thing. So, right from jumpstart, I didn't trust him. My immediate answer was, "Fuck that!" you'll narc me off to Ron and Dorothy. Well somehow he convinced me he wouldn't and I made him promise to let me hang out. So I showed him how to inhale and of course I'm pretty cocky, blowing it real slow through my nose and mouth on the exhale, cause it's kind of funny to me...here I am barely eleven showing this big dumb jock how to inhale a cigarette. I hand it back to him..."Here, now you try." He takes it and I notice right off the bat, he's "nigger-lippin" it, but I don't say anything because I want to see him cough. This is my first chance to make fun of the guy and not get my ass kicked, besides, I just have to see it, and sure enough, hack, hack, hack, hack! The guy almost dies. While he's hacking away, I'm holding my belly gasping for air, laughing my ass off. When he finally stops hacking and I regain my composure, I look at him and say, "You're weird." "How do you do that", he demands. Like a smart ass, I light up another cigarette and doing my best John Wayne impersonation. I say, "Well first of all pilgrim, there's no need to nigger-lip it" and then I exhale a big white cloud into his face. Surprisingly he just lit up another and kept trying until he didn't cough any more. What a trooper, cuz I think we smoked a whole pack that day in the back yard before heading off to hang out at his buddies house...just so we could hang out in the dudes room and guess what...smoke more cigarettes. What a bunch of weenies. Even so, that day was the birth of "Rick", the incredible cigarette vending machine. Before then I would spend all day at the bowling alley in Westgate Mall, trying to work up the nerve to run up to the cigarette machine, pump in my dollar sixty, select my brand and make a fast exit before some grown up spotted me and yelled, "Hey you!"

I had just barely turned eleven in the summer of 1978, but I had already been kicked out of mainstream classes and had been admitted into a class that specifically dealt with kids who had behavioral problems. The teacher in charge of the class was a man by the name of Marty M. His assistant was a woman of the name Sandy S. The class was based on a system of silver and gold stars. If you completed an assignment and got an A or a B, you got 1 small gold star. Four small gold stars equaled 1 big gold star. Four assignments per week for a month with an A or B grade average meant 4 big gold stars at the end of the month, in which case the student would receive a framed Gold Star Authentic Certificate of Completion. Under the same premises for a C or D GPA, a student would receive a framed Silver Star Certificate. This was cool. It gave me something to work toward. At first, as a result of my disruptive behavior, somebody had decided it might be best if I had a male teacher, but I didn't see it that way. We bumped heads until one day I challenged ole Marty to a bat fight. To my astonishment the guy accepted and asked me when and where. I told him to meet me out in front of the school at three o'clock. I had no intention of showing and have no idea if he ever showed, because it was never again discussed. After that I worked exclusively with Sandy S. It was about that time when my interest in music exploded. At home we had a piano and I began to experiment with singing and playing at the same time. I would sit and play from the time I got out of school until it was time to go to bed. It must have driven the entire family insane, but no one ever said a word. I think they were all just happy that I had found another preoccupation, as opposed to terrorizing the family. I was absolutely obsessed with learning how to play the piano. I needed a way to sing my musical thoughts and fast. I quickly realized that I had a great talent for improvising words. I could make up words as I went along about anything I wanted with ease. Day after day, hour upon hour, until my hands hurt, I would play. I was hypnotized by the sound and a need that can't be explained by mere words alone. Finally I felt confidant that I could play to an audience, so I signed up to perform at the school talent show. I was in sixth grade when I received my first standing ovation at that talent show. I haven't the slightest recollection of what I played, but I know it was all adlibbed and improvised. To this day I am still approached by people who say, "You're Randy Snowball aren't you? I remember you from the Eastside Elementary talent show." Sometimes it's a little spooky, but it's always a great honor to think that I could have had such a lasting impact on so many lives.

Shortly after that talent show, I started 7th grade and Junior High. I met my first girlfriend, Sharon, in junior high. She was a ninth grader and we met in that little circle of friends that always meet back behind the school, way out in the field to smoke cigarettes and pot, once before class in the morning and always at lunch. She had her eye on me for sometime. Her approach was, "So you're Randy Snowball, huh? Why don't you skip your bus ride home today and take my bus home with me, my parents don't come home until the evening. What do ya say?" What was I suppose to say? No, I don't think so! This chick was gorgeous, so when three o'clock rolled around, you can bet your ass I was sitting right next to her on her bus. We got off at her stop, walked to her house and fucked. Sharon would definitely fall under the category of "one of the best girlfriends in a lifetime." She was funny, fun, she loved sex, she was loyal and she loved our being together. She also had an appetite for adventure and there were many times when I didn't quite make it out of her room before her parents came home. I would often hide in her closet until the coast was clear enough to either slip out the front door or climb out the window and down the tree that grew along the side of the house. But I wasn't always so lucky. On one occasion I snuck out late and went to Sharon's. I wasn't sure how to get her attention, so I started throwing rocks at her window. It got her attention, but she wasn't the only one. I started talking to her and she says, "Come on, get in here." As I get about halfway up the tree and I hear, "FREEZE RIGHT WHERE YOU ARE!" I look to see who it is…and it's Sharon's Dad…and the guys got a gun on me. So I climb out of the tree and the guy walks me into his house at gunpoint. He sits me down at the kitchen table and proceeds to tell me how lucky I am that I wasn't shot. He calls Sharon into the kitchen and asks if she knows me. "Of course I know him, he's my boyfriend Randy

Snowball...Dad!" With that he asks my phone number and calls Dorothy and Ron to retrieve me. I can still remember hearing them commenting about how loony they thought Sharon's Dad was. Sadly, about a month after that incident, Sharon moved to Newport Beach and I never saw her again. In my view, at the time, it was just another prime example of love's deceptive nature.

After Sharon moved my attitude really went downhill. As a matter of fact I got kicked out of the entire school district for making death threats to the Vice Principal. I was suspended for a long time...but during that time, Dan and I had a blast. I remember one day I came up with the bright idea of parachuting off the roof of the house by tying four pieces of rope to the corners of a "twister" mat. That little fucker must have been laughing his ass off as I sat poised on that rooftop..."ready", "set", "jump"...and down I came like a lead sinker. My landing completely knocked the wind out of me and I thought I was going to die. Needless to say, I never did that again. Dan was my best friend, but he wasn't above revenge. One day we were out front riding our bikes along with a bunch of other kids from the neighborhood. We had set up a milk crate jump in the center of the cul-de-sac and were all taking turns doing jumps. When it came to my turn to jump, I got going as fast as I could. I was way up there in the air when I looked down and saw my front tire fly off. There wasn't anything I could do except land and when I did...my back tire hit the ground...my front forks stuck into the hot soft asphalt...I flipped completely upside down and landed flat on the top of my head. It must have looked pretty funny because I was still in the riding position with my ass on the seat and my feet on the pedals, just stuck in that position until I fell over sideways and ran bawling into the house. Ya know...for fifteen years I told that story on numerous occasions in Dan's presence until one day, after telling the story, he took me aside and confessed to loosening the bolts on my front tire. That son-of-a-bitch had been getting the last laugh on me each time he heard me tell the story over a fifteen year time span. "FUCKER!" He said it was his revenge for me picking on him that week. As I started to get a little older, Dan and I began to sort of grow apart. We had different friends, mostly due to the fact that Dan wasn't involved in the extra curricular activities that I was. I smoked pot and did drugs and snuck out and stole from stores. Dan didn't.

I had a friend named Tom L who had a brother working the graveyard shift at the local 7-11. I use to sneak out at night and walk up to the store to help him stock the cooler in exchange for a couple of cases of beer. He had a second job as a custodian at the BSU Little Theater, so we would go there and drink, playing music over the PA while cleaning the place. Making it from my house to the store was quite literally a game of cat and mouse. Ya see...there was a cop named Officer L, who's beat included the streets between my house and the 7-11. In one week he busted me four times en-route to see my friend. One time, I had barely made it into the store as my friend spotted his patrol car pulling into the store parking lot. He shouted, "In the cooler, in the cooler!" I ran into the cooler and hid in the corner behind some stacks of beer. I waited for the door buzzer...ding-dong, ding-dong. I heard him ask my friend if he'd seen me. My friend said, "Nope." Officer L asked if he could take a look in the cooler, "Sure go ahead." He opened the door to the cooler and just stood there for what seemed an eternity, but then just closed the door and went on his way. Later that week, I was arrested for shoplifting at Smiths Food King. It was Officer L who took the call and on the way to juvenile detention he looked over at me and said, "I knew you were in the cooler that night 'cause I saw ya in the corner." He never did say why he chose to let me go and I didn't ask. Some things are better left alone.

13

After getting arrested for shoplifting, I was assigned a probation officer. My new probation officer's name was Glenn E. He was cool, but I had no intension of abiding by the stipulations of my probation. I met a kid across the street who brought me to his house one day. We were checking out his pellet gun when he asked me if I wanted to see something cool. What was I supposed to say, "No?" He opens the door to a hallway closet and pulls out three, .30-06 hunting rifles, all equipped with high-powered scopes. We took turns looking through the scopes and then returned them to the closet. The next day, while he was in school, I went over to his house and tried the front door. It was unlocked and no one was home. So I went straight to the closet, opened the door and there they were. I grabbed all three and proceeded out the door and across the street, to my house. At first I tried to hide them in the attic under the insulation, but then decided I wanted to check 'em out, so I moved them downstairs. One night, while being watched by a sitter, I had my stereo all the way up as I often did when I listened to music. I was aiming at a spot on the wall, looking through one of the scopes; I pulled the trigger and BAM!!! I could have sworn I unloaded the fuckin thing...but no, I shot holes through the sheet rock in my closet, through both sides of the hallway walls and into the basement concrete wall under the stairs. When the sitter came running down to see what the sound was, the hall was misty with a haze of plaster. Somehow, I managed to convince her that I had lit an M80. As for the holes in the wall, I said they'd always been there and since she had never been to that part of the house, she bought it. If not for my stereo blaring I'd have been in trouble. A few days later a couple of detectives paid me a visit. They said they had received a call from an off duty cop who happened to be driving by as I was crossing the street with what appeared to be three high powered rifles. I said I didn't know anything about that. They left a card and asked me to call if I learned anything. Later that evening, Dorothy and a new acquaintance of hers, who just happened to be a member of a sheriff's posse, approached me. They sat me down and told me I wouldn't get in any trouble if I just gave the guns back. So I did, and believe it or not, that was the end of it.

It was about this time that Dorothy and Ron had separated for good, which in my opinion meant I could do whatever the fuck I wanted…and that's exactly what I did. Eventually Dorothy would have to put the house up for sale so that we could all move into a rental, located within a school district that would accept me. But not just yet. One rainy day shortly before that relocation, Dorothy had a meeting to attend, or something of the sort, where kids weren't allowed or maybe it was just me. I wasn't exactly the kind of kid you could count on to wait patiently in the hall or the car or anywhere. In any case, the decision was made that I would be dropped at a local theater for the afternoon matinee and picked back up after the show. As always, I would play like I was going to the show, but as soon as Dorothy would pull away and be out of sight, I would do an about face and begin a detailed exploration of the area. This included a sweep for chicks, any store with a cigarette machine would be noted, and of course, any other kids my age that were roaming the area. Since neither one of my brothers nor any of the kids in my neighborhood seemed to show much of an appetite for rebellion, I had set out to find me some new friends that could meet or exceed the level of distain I felt for authority…and I found just that in a kid waiting for the city bus that day.

It was weird; it was like we were drawn to each other. I saw him from across the street and when our eyes met it was like we had known each other our entire lives. We traded head nods and as I waited for the light to change at the pedestrian xing we sorta sized each other up and though I had never met this kid in my entire life, I felt no apprehension about approaching him. When I reached the bus bench, I simply sat down and said, "Hey, what's up?" "Not much man, what's up with you?" and he kind of giggled when he said it. I looked at his eyes and that's when I said, "You're stoned, huh?" He giggled some more and I said, "Man you are so busted! You are so stoned, got any more? What's your name?" "Name's Tim, Tim G." Here (as he hands me a little wooden pipe), "What's your name?" "Randy, Randy Snowball", and with that I thought the guy was going to die laughing. He was laughing so hard; I started laughing at the way he was laughing. I wasn't even stoned but it must have been a contact high 'cause we were both goofy. Right about then we both noticed the bus approaching. I tried to hand him his pipe back, but he said, "Keep it." I said, "You're pretty cool, what's your number?" He yelled it out, got on the bus and waved goodbye. I still had a little time to kill and spent it looking for a way to light that bowl and mumbling his number so I wouldn't forget. I had to wait until I got home to get stoned and, although I had memorized his number, it still took weeks before I would work up the nerve to dial it. It was like I was preparing myself to be cool enough because during those weeks I was all strung out on music.

I was just beginning to listen to "music." Ya see, before the age of twelve, the only albums I owned were the Beatles and Pink Floyd's, Dark Side of the Moon and Wish You Were Here. There was no Queen, no Van Halen; oh wait, there was Kiss, but by 1979 they were making way for bands like Bad Company, Styx, Peter Frampton, Ted Nugent, Boston and the Cars, AC/DC and Supertramp. There was an explosion of new music all introducing itself to me at the same time. Much of that music is the kind of music that would set the standard for years to come. When I tell you I was fanatical about music and singing and learning to play that piano, I mean it by every true sense of the word. I mean I'd be riding in the car with Dorothy and a certain song would come on the radio and I would turn it way up and say, "Right there, see! Ya hear that! Wait a minute; here it comes…right there!!! Oh man, I love that part."

14

I was a fuckin freak I tell ya and while we're on the subject of riding in the car with Dorothy, I seemed to always do screwy shit to terrorize her. Sometimes, if she had to run me to school early in the morning, I would sneak out to the car and turn the radio all the way up, the windshield wipers on high, the heater fan on high...just everything. Then I would sneak back into bed and fake like I wasn't getting up. She'd be in a hurry to get me to school on time, hop in, turn the key and "God Dammit Randy." Or how about the time she picked me, Dan and Dan's friend Paul up from Skateland. Well, I had to pee and while she was yelling, "I'm almost there", I'm already pissin out the passenger window as she's driving down the road yelling..."GOD DAMMIT RANDY!" I think I saw her chuckle in the mirror on that one.

Yeah, I would love to do stuff like bum a cigarette or a light from someone in traffic...funny! One of the things (out of many) I will always be forever grateful to Dorothy for is the respect she has always shown for my music during those years I was teaching myself to play and sing. Not one time did she ever come in and say, "Randy, could you keep it down" or "You can't play while I'm trying to work"...not once. As a result she was often audience to some of the best lyrical improvisational compositions of my lifetime. Countless times it would be just the two of us in the house and not a word would be spoken between us as I would play and sing she would be working in a room she called her "office." She really wasn't one of those sit and watch types, and thank God for that, 'cause I was never really one who liked being watched. I didn't mind being heard, but I didn't like being watched.

Finally came the day I decided it was time to call this Tim G character. So I call him up and guess what...he's stoned! Not only is the guy stoned, but he's got some friends over and they've got some booze, they're getting drunk! WOW! I had never had friends that I could actually hang out with, smoke pot, cigarettes, drink booze with and just generally laugh and party with. I'd never been anywhere besides the little adventures I would take whenever dropped off at the movies, but I had an incredible curiosity to see what was going on out there (in the world). It was the kind of arrogant indestructible curiosity more commonly found in kids between the ages of fifteen to nineteen. It just started for me around twelve. I didn't know how, but I was going to get to Tim's. I could tell they were having a good time on the phone. I could hear the music and the laughing and Tim's friend Tom had a sister. As curious as I was and as desperate as I may have been to get there, I still had zero geographical understanding of the city. I didn't know East from West or North from South. Street names meant nothing, so directions were useless. Joining the party would have to wait for me, at least until Friday. Tim assured me that the party would still be going on and especially on Friday. I asked him for the main cross streets near his house and he replied, "Just call me from M & W on 8th Street when you get a ride and I'll come meet ya." I didn't know it at the time, but this was perfect because Dorothy worked downtown, not far from this location, and I could catch a ride and have her drop me off. She said she would pick me up after work, but I had no intention of meeting her. The thing with me was, that if I started from home and went somewhere, I could always find my way back... no matter what. I would come home when I was ready or when I got hungry. I was arrogant and desperate to get away. The move from California pissed me off and I had made my mind up that I was going to do whatever I wanted, whenever I wanted. Finally, Friday came around; it was the summer of 1979. I couldn't get Dorothy to just drop me off at the store, so Tim gave me directions to his house from M & W. It was only about 3 blocks away and easy to find. As soon as Dorothy knew which house and where, there was no problem. I'm sure she was happy to see that I had made new friends because, quite frankly, if I wasn't playing the piano or listening to my stereo on 10, it meant I was up to an evil deed. The first thing we did at my new friend Tim's was meet his Mom and borrow her bong. She was way cool and I immediately admired their relationship. After some observation, and about an hour of getting stoned and listening to music in Tim's room (all the while keeping Mom in my peripheral), I had to ask myself "the question."

72

Was this the kind of relationship I might have had with my Mom? You see, though I had only been with my natural mother for the first five years of my life, it was long enough for me to absorb a conscious acknowledgement of her lifestyle. It was that conscious acknowledgement that made it possible for me to identify the similarities between Tim's Mom and my own natural Mother, thus enabling me to conclude that my Mom was a "stoner" (partier). But it was more than that. I had the same chemistry with Tim's Mom as with Tim. Some people you meet you're just cool with from day one. Anyway, we returned Mom's bong and headed out the door, "Goin' to Tom's, see ya later", Tim would say.

15

Tom R, where and how does one begin to describe a kidlike Tom? Well let's start like this, "knock, knock, knock!" (commotion and music in the background) (Tom's Mom) "Who is it?" (Tim) "It's Tim and Randy Snowball." "Who?" (Tom cutting in front of Mom to open the door) "God"...Mom, let 'em in! It's Tim and his new friend Randy Snowball...just let 'em in...jeezus! Ya know, I don't know why but both Tim and Tom would always introduce me, as Randy Snowball, not just Randy, not just Snowball, but Randy Snowball. Anyway, Mom steps aside as Tom let's us in, stereo blaring, television on, Tom rolling his eyes as Mom does her best to emphasize that there will be no parties in Rose's room tonight. (Tom) "You guys are eating, right?" (As Tom's Mom rolls her eyes.) Just then Tom sticks a plate in each of our hands and that's when I see it. Buried behind the kitchen table and some chairs is an antique upright piano. I'm fixated by it. There's a reason for this. The reason is because everything I knew and learned up to that point was on only one piano. The only other pianos I had ever laid hands on were Grannies (Dorothy's Mom), which happens to be identical to Dorothy's, and the school piano at the talent show. So whenever I see a piano somewhere, even to this day, I'm drawn to it...because playing piano is like driving a car, they each have their own unique feel. We ate dinner and immediately after I asked to play it. Now I didn't know it at the time, but this Tom R kid, as I would come to learn in later years, equals if not surpasses the degree of passion for music that I have. So I sit down and start to play and something truly magical sets in. The television is clicked off, the stereo is turned off and suddenly you can hear a pin drop in an environment that just moments before was chaotic.

As I write this now, I am compelled to confess that it was not until recent years that I have actually been capable of regarding this and many other experiences with regard to my music in the same light as others. In my experience thus far however, I have discovered, at least in my case, that with age I have no doubt acquired a much broader capacity for appreciation than my capabilities to take it for granted. In other words, I can only take talent for granted for so long until enough time passes that I can't help but notice that not everyone can do what I do with such ease, and it's at that point when I had wished I'd known sooner.

I played the piano at Tom's house for about an hour during which time Tom's sister Rose came out of her room. I only know this from hearing the sound of her bedroom door open and close as my back was to it as I played, but when I was done, it was only Tom and me there. I'm certain I would have only played a short medley of things I knew had it not been for the mood of the room and a unique talent that Tom had for "speechless prodding." Tom R would become one of the few people I would enjoy having watch me play. He really seemed to hang on every word and I feel it's a great honor to play for someone who really appreciates the music with such heart. It sure beats the hell outta playing for someone who could care less, wouldn't you agree? Obviously, Tom and I would become friends instantly. When I was done, we headed for Rose's room and there sat Tim and Rose drinking Madd Dog 20/20 and smoking Marlboro 100's. Rose was butt ugly, just kidding, "Had ya going though didn't I Rose." It's just that I know that someday you're going to read this and it's the best way I could think of to both exemplify the kind of relationship we have and communicate my love for you at the same time. As you know, I wouldn't make fun if I didn't love you and your family to death. Rose and I hit it off immediately, but it's important to note that it wasn't so much a boyfriend, girlfriend relationship, though that's not to say we weren't attracted to each other. There were many times we would spend locked in her room just kissing and embracing, sometimes tickling one another, laughing, sometimes even arguing, but only when the booze ran out. That was as sexual as it ever got between Rose and I. Rose was a little older than me, so I think it was a combination of my being a lot younger than I looked, and a complicated mutual apprehension that neither one of us was going to allow it to get as serious as we both knew it could get. By the way, Rose is anything "but" ugly, quite the contrary in fact.

I spent the weekend at Tim's and since I had missed my ride with Dorothy (stood her up), I walked home when it came time to go. It's not as if I couldn't have called her for a ride, but let's face it, "I'll see you guys later", sounds a lot cooler than, "Mommy's on her way", doesn't it? Besides, I knew I was in trouble, but even still I looked forward to what I had already convinced myself to believe would be the "adventurous challenge" of making it home. The mileage meant nothing to me. I knew it was far, but that only added to the anticipation of the adventure. As I walked I realized I could have been hitch hiking, but I decided against it.

I had a great need to familiarize myself with the city streets, not so much geographically, but the feel of them. The look in the eyes of each passerby was a curious thing to me, whether it is by those people in cars or someone walking down the street, it really didn't matter. I wanted to see faces and I wanted my face to be seen. I wanted to know what kinds of reactive expressions I received and also what kinds of expressive reactions came from me. One of the things that I experienced in public schools in my interaction with teachers, as well as with many of my peers, was the tendency to be misinterpreted as being mad or having an attitude. Ninety percent of the time I was and I did have an attitude, but for the other 10 percent of that time, in all honesty and from the heart of my soul I tell you this, not only was I not mad and didn't want an attitude, but I wanted desperately to stop the madness and attitude of the monster I had perpetuated through my facade. Unfortunately, I had already perpetuated the beast and that 10 percent would have been impossible for anyone to know about. I know it now, but I didn't know it then, and as a result I was misinterpreted as having an attitude at times when I didn't by teachers who thought they were going to be disciplinarians. So ya know what I did with that 10 percent? I experimented with it on long walks by exposing myself to people in society who had absolutely no knowledge of the beast I had perpetuated at home. With society I didn't have to be mad because that's what was expected of me. But at home, I had created such a reputation for being non-compliant and defiant that I didn't have the know how or even the intellectual strength at that age to overcome it. There was still the nagging question of what had happened to my natural Mother. The great distance from my sister fueled the beast of my defiance. And that I couldn't just "stop" being mad about it all made me a powder keg at home...so the longer the walk home, the more time I had to experiment and explore that 10 percent of passive natural curiosity I was experiencing.

But when I got home I was busted. Every time I did this, it was a violation of my probation. I wouldn't always know I was busted at first because I didn't know how it worked. For example, in the beginning of what would soon be extensive career as a juvenile delinquent, I had no idea that the conversations between my PO and Dorothy would ultimately be the deciding factor on whether or not I would be incarcerated in juvenile detention or not. So as a result, my first couple of scheduled visits left me feeling a bit betrayed by Dorothy. I began to aim all my hostilities directly at Dorothy. My first experiences in detention were a direct result of her betrayal as far as I was concerned, which made me extremely volatile with her a lot of the time. There were times I would explode just like a powder keg and begin to destroy everything in sight. She would restrain me to the best of her physical ability, I would struggle away, thrashing about, she would restrain me again and this would continue all the while me screaming at the top of my lungs, "I HATE YOU!" and her screaming back, "Well that's just too bad, 'cause I love you"! Back and forth and back and forth, until we both became to exhausted to fight anymore. Her sitting on my arms and legs, both of us crying, with me still panting out between breaths, "I hate you!" and her panting, "Too bad! That's not going to work, 'cause I love you!" She would say, "You can hate me all you want, but I'm still going to love you!" And ya know what I'd say? I'd say, "I don't care, cuz I hate you!"

I started hitchhiking to Tom's to hang out with Tim, Tom and Rose, but before long Rose violated her probation and was sent away to reform school. Shortly after that happened, Tom moved out of his Mom's into a little house that was located on the same property. Tim learned that he would be moving to Eugene, Oregon, but not before he would introduce me to my new girlfriend. Her name was Carol B and she was fun and beautiful and horny. We really didn't go out for very long since she eventually would move to Apache Junction, but man was she fun! My sole reason for even mentioning Carol is that though our time together was short, it was one of the happiest times of my life. Carol B was so gorgeous and vibrant that just being with her made me feel incredible about myself. Nothing was ever too serious, not that everything was a joke either. The environment was completely drama free in our relationship. In fact, Carol and I would just, out of nowhere, come up with these ad-libbed improvisational skits about what it would be like to be in one of those high drama relationships. Ya know like she would come spinning out of her room dressed like Julie Andrews singing, "The hills are alive with the sound of Music", she'd fall into my arms and without missing a beat, I would start in with, "I am sixteen", (Carol) "Going on seventeen." We would both burst out in laughter and end up making out, just kissing passionately on the couch for long periods of time. You know.........dry humping' until we couldn't stand it anymore and would make our way up to her room and well you know. It was a very sexual relationship! Anyway, the week Carol told me her family would be moving to Arizona, I got picked up downtown by the cops for curfew and did 30 days for probation violation. I never got out in time to say goodbye and never saw her again.

"Devastated?" an understatement, but par-for-the-course in my mind. I quickly became very well known in the Ada County Detention Center between countless stints and the 30 days I spent there. I had acquired myself a notorious reputation as a Human Radio/Comedian. I began to discover the pluses and minuses of having a name like "Snowball." Everyone knew who I was because you couldn't forget the name. I was a fascinating character and had an admirable personality, compounded with my musical ability and a memory that enabled me to recall the lyrics from every song on many entire albums. I became well known for providing entertainment for all my cellmates as well as much of the staff. The Ada County Detention Center was co-ed and I had been there so many times that I had begun to establish the foundations for friendships with kids I would know for the rest of my life. Each time I would get busted and have to go to the detention Center for a stay, it became more like a reunion. It seemed to always be the same girls and the same boys and as a result we all became friends.

One of the things I would do to increase my own popularity was exploit my name in detention. I learned how to do this after getting suspended from school for a couple of days. When I came back to school I noticed that my name had preceded me. So whenever I was in detention, I would make a point of drawing attention to myself so that everyone would hear my name. In every institution I've ever experienced, prisoners are commonly addressed as "Mr. so and so." In my case "Mr. Snowball." It was Mr. Snowball this, or Mr. Snowball that, all the time and each time every head in the place would turn. Now In order to accomplish this, it meant I had to break a lot of rules and I was good at that, but I was also smart enough to know that it could be done without having to compromise my popularity or what had become long-standing relationships with staff. I found ways of doing it without violence and without the sacrifice of good rapport. I was a "singing clown", although there was an occasional hostile confrontation from time to time. I never made any enemies with staff, but lets face it, I still had some serious issues with authority. Eventually it was my clowning, mixed with an unpredictable temper that could be quite volatile at times, that led to my ending up in solitary confinement. I still had a lot of anger and resentment due to the unanswered questions in my life, but also as a direct result of my own inadvertent creation of a "facade" that I didn't know how to kill. I really resented it when in situations I couldn't control no one had the decency to offer any explanation for why things had to be the way they had to be. "WHY!" I would often cry in a fit of rage as I looked up to the sky with fists clenched cursing God. "WHAT DID I DO? WHAT? WHAT DID I DO?" With my face beat red, tears streaming down my face, one fist clenched and the other in the "FUCK YOU" position flipping off the sky, I would scream at the very top of my lungs, looking up…"FUCK YOU!! FUCK!! FUCKIN' YOU!!" It wasn't even so much that I didn't like myself; it was more that I had grown up to count on being let down by the people closest to me. I just wasn't going to let anyone "get" close to me and that's all there was to it. It wasn't a matter of thinking I wasn't worthy of anyone's love; it was that I knew I was, but I was continually made a fool of for thinking so. So what do you do when you keep being made a fool of? Well, eventually you go to any extent to not let it happen again, and I was an expert at doing this. Above all, I wanted to love and I wanted to be able to let people love me. I knew Dorothy loved me, but I didn't know how to let that happen. I kept getting bomb barded with all this low self-esteem crap from psychologists and Dorothy was buying into it, and who wouldn't? But the fact is that I had become buried by my own frustrations, helplessness and confusions. I wasn't *asked* how I felt most of the time, I was *told* how I felt, and even if I had been asked, there's just no way I could have just simply called all the adults together for a quick conference. What would I have said? "Uh... okay let's loose the shrink and uh... by the way, what's the status on that people search for Becky C?" Any word back from Google? I mean come on it's taken me this long just to put it into words and "Google" didn't exist back then so, let's get back to reality! (whatever that is).

16

It was at about this time that we moved from the house on Woodside Ct. into a three-story rental on a street called Primrose Lane. As I mentioned earlier, it was the only way I could go to school since I had been excluded from our previous school district. We had to move into an entirely new school district and the name of my new school was Lincoln. Now Lincoln was a school whose student body consisted of all the kids from all the other schools who had been expelled with no possibility of re-enrollment, as well as kids suffering from mental retardation and physical handicaps. The principal of this school was an ex-boxer. At this point in his life, he was an old pudgy bald man and his name was Mr. N. I got kicked out the first day for throwing a chair at my new teacher Mr. B, but I returned the next day as a result of Dorothy threatening to call my probation officer. I went back and got into a fight with a kid, who kicked my ass by pulling the hood of my jacket over my head as he proceeded to uppercut me. When Mr. N broke it up, he said if we wanted to fight we could take it in the gymnasium and put the gloves on. We agreed and took it to the gym. Right off the bat the guy knocks the wind out of me and as I'm trying' to catch my breath the guy almost gets another couple of shots in before Mr. N is able to get between us, but not quite. As I'm sitting' there catching my breath, Mr. N keeps asking' me, "Had enough, have ya had enough?" Well, my mind is saying' "Fuck yea, I've had enough!" but there was no way I was going to be the new chair throwing' kid who pussed out in two punches, so I catch my breath and Mr. N steps aside. We start to square off and the kid starts coming' at me again and just out of natural reaction, I kick him in the mouth and he goes down. Right about then I feel this vice like grip on the back of my neck and its Mr. N. "That ain't fair fighting' Mr. Snowball! Are you all right?" Looking down at the kid, Mr. N saw that he had a split lip, but other than that he was all right. Mr. N let go of my neck and as the kid got up, he handed him a towel for the blood and made us shake hands. On our way back down the hall, away from Mr. N, the kid introduced himself as John, John F. He stuck his hand out, I took it and began my introduction, but he interjected with, "Randy Snowball, I know, good meeting ya." And after that we had no problems.

One of the things about Lincoln was that the buses that took everyone home after school were already half filled with older Vo-tech students by the time they had arrived to pick us up. The ironic part about that was that a lot of those kids were kids I knew from detention. Since my house was one of the last stops, I got a chance to see where many of them lived. I collected a lot of phone numbers from friends I normally only ever saw in detention. Those friends had friends that had either already known me or knew of me. On the weekends we would all congregate downtown for the "cruise." Our favorite place to hang out was a parking lot behind a restaurant called The Royal Fork. We would all just hang around there listening to the music from car stereos. At that time, the music most commonly heard was music from bands like The Eagles, The Cars, Boston, Rush, Pink Floyd, Bad Company, Ted Nugent, AC/DC...I think you get the idea. Anyway, we (our little group) would all meet at Tom's and pool our money to get alcohol and we'd get as drunk as we could. The first time we did this, Tom and Tim introduced me to a new character in the clan. His name was Tom D. Tom was fun. Very fun! and we hit it off right from the moment we met. What I liked about these guys was that nobody wanted to kick anybody's ass. Nobody had anything to prove, except for maybe how much booze we could drink. There was one thing Tom D and I would commonly compete at and that was who could run faster from the cops or who could run faster from the store clerk during a "beer run." A "beer run" was just that; walk in, grab a case or two and run! Tom could run just a little bit faster, but I had the record for how much beer in one night...4 cases. We only did this when nobody had any money. When we finally got drunk enough, usually it would be just me and Tom D that would head downtown and cruise for chicks or just walk around talking to people we knew.

There was one night in particular when Tim decided not to be such a homebody and join us. We three made our way toward downtown, as Tom's was only a couple of blocks from the main loop. We made it to the parking lot behind the Royal Fork and were hanging out, each of us in our own little group in separate areas of the lot. Tim had been hanging out with a group nearest to a delivery door at the rear of the restaurant sort of in an alley. Well, apparently Tim thought it would be funny to keep ringing the delivery bell at the back door. The next thing I knew, I'm looking over at where Tim was standing and I see this fella dressed in all white wearing one of those big chef hats. He's holding a big butcher knife in one hand and Tim's hair in the other. Apparently, the head Chef had enough delivery bells for one night. A lot of people started to move toward the door and as soon as he let go of Tim's hair, Tim vacated and the Chef barely got the door shut as a barrage of beer bottles smashed against it. The three of us knew the cops would be there soon so we got out of the area and began to make our way back to Tom R's house. We were all pretty drunk and on the way back I got an idea. I knew of a building that was currently being renovated. It was one of the old historic downtown buildings and it had one of those snooty little fancy pants restaurants in it, and it was still pretty early so I knew the doors would still be open. It was called the Hoff Building. I use to go there with Carol B. The renovation included a fancy glass roof that was still under construction. You could go up there and look at people and stuff from way up high and I discovered it on one of my exploration walks home. It was like a big rooftop café before they put the glass in. Carol and I would go up there sometimes and make out. Good ole Carol, but Carol was gone now so I figured what the hell, it was time to desecrate it's secrecy. Well, we get there and sure enough it's open. We hit the elevator and headed for the top floor. We all stepped out, milled around, peered over the edge, tried spitting on a few pedestrians (Tom's idea, I swear) and then we made a curious discovery. There was another elevator, a freight elevator. It was brand new and designed to bring inventory and supplies up to the new rooftop restaurant, which wasn't open as yet. We all looked at each other and stepped into it. We didn't know where the doors would open to or whom we would face once we got there, but like I said, we were all having a pretty good time that night. We hit the "B" button and held our breath. When it stopped, we all prepared ourselves for sort of a break and run situation, even though we hadn't really done anything wrong...yet. We were relieved and surprised to find no one in sight when the door opened. One look and we knew where we were, in the kitchen of this fancy pants restaurant. Tim just wanted to get out of there, but Tom and I, being of a more criminal mind, decided we better have a look around and that's when we found it...the cooler, filled with booze. Have you ever seen the look on the faces of those two kids on a Jiffy Pop wrapper? Well, go ahead and picture that for a minute and then try to imagine the expressions on those faces instantly changing into the expressions on the faces of people watching a horror movie, because that's exactly what our faces did when the alarm on that emergency door went off when Tim opened it. Oh Man! We had to think fast, so we each grabbed a gallon of Carlo Rossi Burgundy in each hand and just barely made it out of there. We grabbed four gallons and hid out in a church in the window well for an hour as cops drove around looking for us. We all puked Burgundy wine that weekend and I'll never touch that stuff again.

There was another group of friends I use to hang with. The relationship with these friends originated in detention, as a result of our seeing each other time after time. We were easily the most well known residents in the facility at that time. The names of these friends were Rueben C and Pee Wee (Michael) G. The only places we really ever saw each other were at a local skating rink called Skateland, detention, sometimes downtown at the Cruz or at the fairgrounds during the County Fair. We would often see each other at these places and got along well. Our reputations preceded us before we actually met. Rueben and Pee Wee hung out together most of the time, rather than the three of us. They were a little older than me, which meant they had better connections. You see the three of us had sort of a little business arrangement and it all sort of hinged on our popularity. It started downtown at the Cruz when someone I knew wanted some pot. Well, it just so happened that i knew these two characters were selling' pot, dime bags, 8th's, whatever. I would get the money and go track them down and then return to the customer with the product. Pretty soon I became well known for being the guy who could get whatever you wanted; Pot, Hash, Mushrooms, Acid, but I never had any requests for Cocaine, Meth, or Heroin, so I didn't mess with any of them.

17

The best time of the year, for us, was the County Fair. By the time it came around the first year, I was already well known by a shit load of people in the circle. In fact, more people knew of me than I knew of them. Once again, my name had preceded me, making me the perfect distributor. Between the three of us, we probably sold at least 5000 hits of blotter style acid or LSD named Red Dragon at the County Fair. Blotter LSD comes in sheets of perforated paper squares ¼ the size of a postage stamp. Each square of the LSD we were selling had a tiny picture of a red dragon on it, hence the name, "Red Dragon." Sometimes we would get blotter sheets with little black pyramids, called "Black Pyramid." We sold so much of it that it had quickly become the blotter of choice. I don't know where they got it and I didn't care, I just sold it and sold it and sold it, not to mention all the hash and pot people wanted. It was through this time of my life that I established myself as someone who could be trusted with money and large amounts of drugs. A front to Randy Snowball meant a guaranteed payment of cash. I was lucky and well liked enough that I never got ripped off, probably because I never ripped anyone off myself. In fact, I gave buying incentives to return customers and friends out of my own profits. If the price was normally 5 dollars a hit, I'd sell two for $6. I never cared about the money that I could have been making. What was important to me was how great it made me feel when I saw how happy people were to see me. I liked that and I liked the sense of trust people had in me. When my friends saw me they knew they were in for a laugh and that reputation was enough for me. I also ate a lot of the LSD myself. After all, I couldn't sell anything I wouldn't take myself, right? I ate so much acid in fact, that I can't even begin to describe the experiences. Well...maybe one.

In the summer of 1980, it was hotter than hell in Boise, Idaho and I was 13 years old. All week I had been anxiously waiting for a concert. Now, I had been to a few concerts already by this time: Judas Priest, UFO, April Wine, Styx, to name a few, but these shows had all been held inside the exposition building at the fairgrounds. The upcoming concert featured two bands: the opener, Molly Hatchet and the headlining band, Cheap Trick. The show was called the Cheap Trick Dream police tour. Now what made this concert so special was that it was to be held outside in front of a grandstand of a horse track that was located right next to the fairgrounds. On the night of the show I caught a ride with Rueben and Pee Wee. On the way into the car Rueben takes me aside and says, "Hey Snowball" I got a couple of hits of 4-way Blue Spiral, you want to split one? Now, let me tell a little about Rueben C...this is one of those guys with a great talent for persuasion, not only is he persuasive, but he's an extremist. Now throw sneaky in the mix and voila, you've got Rueben C. One of the ways Reuben would get his kicks (I found out the hard way) was to slip you double sometimes, triple what you thought you were taking. This is especially easy to do with a 4-way hit of blotter LSD, because, instead of a paper square ¼ the size of a postage stamp, it's a square the size of a postage stamp perforated into 4. So 1 hit of 4-way LSD is actually 4-hits of the norm...in one. Well, I agree to split one with good ole Rueben, but he says, on one condition. On the condition that we both take it at the same time and wash it down as opposed to chewing on it. So what does he do? Well, instead of tearing one in half (unbeknownst to me at the time) he simply folded it, and said, "1, 2, 3, go!" I didn't even look at it, but I had just eaten a 4-way hit of Blue Spiral.

We got to the concert, walked through the ticket gate and instantly lost track of each other. Oh sure, I would see both Pee Wee and Rueben periodically throughout the show but we were all so caught up in the hallucinations and the laughter that all we could do is give each other the "look" in passing. Now for those of you out there who have never experienced LSD, the "look" is a glance that is exchanged by people that have taken the same LSD at the same party and are at the same stage of the trip. With a glance one might say to the other, "Are you seeing what I'm seeing?" Anyway, the point being rarely does one find a use for words while frying on acid, so the "look" is all part of the experience. This is one of the reasons (of many) that it is no fun frying alone. Without someone to share the extra sensory psychological conformation in the comfort of knowing that there is someone on the same wavelength, there is a tendency to well...shall we say, feel a bit misunderstood. But hey, don't get me wrong, you can take LSD alone, but it's a whole nother ball game. After watching one of the best concerts of my life and having what will be remembered as one of the best times I have ever had, one of the last things I remember is getting into the back seat of a car with some girls. As we pulled out onto the street and began to pick up speed I recall the trails on the painted lines in the road zipping by on both sides of my peripheral vision. But it was nothing compared to being stopped at a red light and as it turned green watching the green light drop onto the hood of the car in the form of a water droplet. I really can't say what happened after that, just that I woke up at a house with a bunch of women of all ages who seemed to know me or at least my name, while I couldn't for the life of me tell ya who any of them were. Yes, I was fully clothed.

The day after that concert it was 113 degrees outside. I was suffering from severe dehydration and I remember the day quite well. I couldn't make it home, had to wait for Dorothy to get off of work, and then be picked up by her for a ride home. What I didn't know was that Dorothy would be picking up Rick and seeing him off to the Army. Oh, I knew he was going but I had no idea when, and at the risk of sounding insensitive, I must say, I didn't care! I really must have suffered a heat stroke that day because I thought I was going to die! Now that I think of it, I'm sure it was more than likely the combination of dehydration, lack of food and strychnine poisoning from the

LSD. Whatever it was, it left me face down on the floorboard of the Suburban like the chalk line at a homicide scene. I couldn't even get up to say goodbye to Rick. Off to Fort Leonard Wood he went.

It took me about a week to recuperate from that concert, but I bounced back with a vengeance. I began to party more and more, taking more and more chances with the law, curfew violations, shoplifting, open container, illegal consumption of alcohol and possession of marijuana. I even snatched a couple of purses, but was never caught for that, which is ironic considering the fact that it was purses that got me busted, again. One time I spent a week stealing purses out of cars. I hadn't finished going through them yet so I carelessly stashed them under my bed where Dorothy discovered them while I was out. I came home, discovered them gone and flipped out on her. Going on about how she had violated my privacy by snooping around my room. Who was I to talk with purses under my bed? Anyway, we had a big fight and I took off. I must have gotten picked up on something, probably curfew, and then violated by my probation officer, because the next thing I remember is being locked up.

18

By this time in my life, I had become an expert in the field of knowing just how far to push "it" and this time was no exception. I had been fuckin' up for a long time, but I had developed a kind of pattern that was perpetual in its downward spiral. I acquired an ability to parallel a capacity for the acceptance of consequences at the time of each perpetrated action. Let me put it this way; if you go to court to be sentenced and think your gonna get a break (leniency) but don't, you're devastated, but if you go under the assumption you'll be getting the max, well then even the smallest break is a pleasant surprise! Which would you rather be psychologically prepared for? The catch 22, I would soon learn, is that you can be aware of the adversity of the consequences for your own actions, but we are all living breathing examples of the fact that being "aware" doesn't always prevent us from making the wrong decision and "knowing" certainly doesn't make the consequence any easier to swallow. Quite the contrary in fact, the pain is in the knowing and I had a lot of pain because I knew exactly what I was doing.

I mentioned earlier in this book that at an early age I had experienced a hell of a lot of hostility toward God, as opposed to myself, for what I believed to be extraordinarily unfair circumstances. It wasn't me I didn't like; it was more of an extreme distain for the way things apparently had to be. However, with age came the responsibility to make more and more decisions for myself, and the choices I'd began to make did in fact ultimately give birth to a brand new introspective resentment. It is at this age that I began to dislike myself for making decisions that I would increasingly be held accountable for. I don't know, I mean sure...I did make a lot of bad choices, but I'd have had to have been a robot to have exercised enough emotional self-control to have made all the right ones. Anyway, I think the best way to sum it up would be...helplessness = defiance, and man did I feel helpless.

Once again I found myself in a single man cell (solitary confinement)...Home Sweet Home! I wasn't allowed to attend the school they had everyone attend during the day and, as a matter of fact, I even had to eat in my cell. I got out for 15 minutes a day to shower and that was it. My probation officer was the coolest P.O. that anyone could hope for. I knew he had a job to do so there were never any hard feelings. On the few visits I had with him, when I hadn't been incarcerated on the spot, we would spend the visit having lunch at McDonalds, as opposed to having our conversations in the dry seriousness of his office. He knew I smoked cigarettes and he didn't mind that I did in his presence, as he was also a smoker. I remember once leaving the drive-thru at McDonalds when he had asked me to empty his overflowing ashtray. He stopped; I slid it out of its compartment, opened my door and tapped it out on the sidewalk. We both burst into laughter when I looked up at the trashcan he'd pulled up next to...oops! I hadn't given it a second thought. I think he said something along the lines of, "You're something else Snowball" as I closed the car door and he pulled out into the street.

Even when I was in juvenile detention, Glen would come and pull me out of my cell and take me into an interview room so I could have a cigarette and we would talk. You know, just kinda "shoot the shit."

Having Glen E as a probation officer was one of the best things that could have happened to me at that age. He knew I wasn't getting out of my cell for most of the time during my stay and although this was a direct result of my defiant and disruptive behavior, he still thought enough of me to take the time out of his busy schedule just to get me out of that cell and cut me some slack. That made me feel like a million bucks, especially the part about having to keep my mouth shut about the smoking. Are any of those kinds of guys around anymore? For the sake of social work I pray that there are.

Throughout many of my stints in juvenile detention, as all throughout my childhood between the ages 6 and upward, I would be introduced into therapy sessions with social workers, psychologists and psychiatrists. "Psychiatric evaluation" had become a phrase introduced into my vocabulary at a very young age, right along with "psychological analysis" and a host of other titles and phrases. I say titles because these were the defining titles attached to the majority of tests I had been asked to take. These tests would often consist of anywhere between 400 to 600 questions. I didn't mind taking them and for an interesting reason. I found that many of the questions asked in those tests were questions I had been dying to be asked for a long time. For example: Do you ever feel unworthy of being heard? Are you afraid of the dark? Do you have feelings of hopelessness? The biggest problem for me however, was that I could only choose 1 out of 3 of the multiple choice answers already provided, which were "yes", "no", or "sometimes." I was furious that I wasn't allowed to select one and then offer my explanation as to why I felt the way I did. It just seemed rude that they had asked me to take this long test, give me only three ways in which to respond, and then, based on my selections, could just take it upon themselves to assume they knew where my head was at. I mean, "Who the fuck did they think they were?" Shouldn't I have an opportunity to explain my answers, I thought to myself? Well, apparently not, and I was not only appalled, but I was insulted! I became even more insulted when after answering a few questions, I had discovered that many of these questions were identical... except worded differently. I mean whom did they think they were dealing with...some moron with no command of the English language? The way I took it was that not only was I being asked to take this very long test that I could only answer in three ways, and being insulted by their disinterest in the "why's" for my selections, but also I was going to have to be sitting across the desk from this jerk-off who would be looking down his nose at me with his text book in one hand and my test results in the other, thinking he knew who the fuck I was. "No fucking way", I thought to myself! Now remember I'm only about the age of 13, but for a 13 year old I have an absolutely incredible memory. Combined with that and the fact that I had taken a lot of the same types of tests over a long period of time, I developed an inevitable mastery in the manipulation of those tests. All right, I'll admit I did get some pleasure in staring back at these "textbook" jerk-offs as they would try and rationalize my psychological evaluation. Just a little! But ya know what, the statistical information in those textbooks have nothing to do with who I am. Based on the answers I provided, I merely dared them to figure out who those "stats" belonged to, and I had a blast watching them try.

It was during this stint in juvenile detention that I had been assigned a new psychologist. Unfortunately, I don't recall his name as I had only two brief sessions with this man before being sent off to reform school. The first of which was our introduction session. I was taken from my cell, introduced to him and then walked to his office in another part of the building. Once there, we were left alone for a one-hour discussion. He was a sort of heavyset man in his early to mid fifties. The guy didn't want any tests, he wasn't holding any textbook and he certainly wasn't looking down his nose at me, though he did have striking eyes with a knowing look that suggested high mileage in his experience of life. I really liked this guy because he talked "with" me and not "at" me. While other psychologists were asking, "How do you feel", he would ask, "What's going on with you?" And instead of threatening reprisals for certain disruptive behaviors, he would say, "Sure...you could do that, but you've been doing that for so long already that you know well enough what will happen. You must be tired, why not try something else", he would say.

This was actually my first experience of being presented with the kind of practical logic that made me stop and think. This is by no means to say that I had not been exposed to this kind of thought process before, but what finally made it work for me was all in the presentation. I liked this guy. He was good! He was smooth and I didn't mind being disarmed by him. His mannerisms suggested to me that he knew where I was coming from, but he still displayed an interest in hearing it and didn't blame me for how I felt.

I recall my impression of him with such clarity, specifically because of the impact of that hour and because of a bizarre circumstance that occurred 3 days later involving him. I received a visit from Dorothy in my cell at the detention center. The purpose of the visit was specific. Dorothy, by this time, was completely at her wits end and distraught about what to do with me. She was frustrated and it pained her to have to see me in such a continued state of turmoil. She had apparently decided that the only course of action left was to try and locate my natural mother and she had come to ask if I thought it might make a difference for me. My response was less than enthusiastic, partly because I was so sure that I had made it clear through my actions that...that was what I had always wanted, partly because

I knew it wouldn't be happening anytime soon because I was ready to be sent to reform school, and at that point in the game I was busy......busy being mad. I told her I didn't care what she did and to get the hell out of my cell! She through her arms up and obliged. After she had gone and I was sure that she was, I began to sob, and on that day I cried and sobbed for longer and harder than I ever had in my life. Clenching my fist and flipping off the sky, cursing God...pounding on the walls and door screaming, "I hate you!" until I had neither the strength nor the will to cry anymore. When I was finally all cried out, I got up and blew all the snot out of my nose and I let my head clear. In that moment of silence it occurred to me to pray, not because I believed God cared enough about me to listen or answer, but because I was convinced he wouldn't and I was out to prove that to myself. I decided that the way I was going to go about doing this was to pray for something very specific, that I would make it fair by praying as hard and as constantly as I could for the rest of the day...and if by sundown my prayers weren't answered, then in my mind I will have proven the nonexistence of God. So there I was, this 13 year old kid, in a 5 by 8 cell, on his hands and knees, praying his brains out for hours and by the end of the day I found myself beginning to feel the first hint of disappointment, not that I was afraid God didn't exist, but that what I was praying for was something I really wanted and it didn't look like I was gonna get it. I had one knee off the floor when I heard the jailer keys jingling all the way down the corridor and as the sound gradually became louder and louder, my palms were sweating, my heart was beating until finally "clink" "clink!" I'll be a son of a bitch if my cell door didn't open up right at sundown and reveal the guy I had taken such a liking to days before (my new psychiatrist) just standing there, arm extended, trying to hand me a Hershey bar. Exactly what I had prayed for. All I could do was stand there dumbfounded until he broke the silence with, "Here, if you don't take it I'm gonna eat it and this Baby Ruth." I slowly reached out still speechless with a trembling hand and took the Hershey. As we both sat silently unwrapping our candy bars on the edge of my bunk, I finally looked over at him and asked *the question*. "So what made you decide to come see me?" His answer was really quite simple. He said, "I don't know, I was sitting at my desk getting ready to go home for the day when I found myself staring at a picture I have on my desk of my wife and children and then felt compelled to come see you." I didn't even ask about the candy bar before he volunteered…"I had to stop for gas on the way and thought you might like a Hershey." I looked at him and said, "Weird." Not another word was spoken about it. The biggest reason I didn't mention how I had prayed for his visit was because God had my mouth stuffed with crow by the guy's presence and the rest of the reason was…well…'cause it's not cool or tough to pray, not when you're trying to be a 13-year-old tough guy. We just kind of shot the shit with small talk for a while. Any efforts on his part to discuss what was going on with Randy were avoided and quickly dismissed by me simply because of the fact that I was already tremendously emotionally and spiritually drained. I'm certain this was observed and acknowledged, as he was very accommodating. I would find out later the reason I now believe he was so relaxed and "on the real" with me. I was a last minute assignment to his caseload just prior to his retirement. He had been asked by Glenn E to look at my file and meet with me.

A few days later I had court. I was escorted into the courtroom, sat down in front of the judge, and I was, to say the very least, "smug." As I have said before, when I'm on a downward spiral I'm well aware of how long it is, so by the time I hit bottom, I'm ready to go! When all the procedural formalities were finally said and done the judge just kinda sat there in exasperation looking down his nose at me. *Nothing*, at that time in my life, could make my blood boil more, so I just glared back at him with all the hate and discontent I could muster. Now I can't recall what the exact exchange of words between that judge and me were, but I can tell you it went something like this. Judge: You do realize Mr. Snowball that based on these charges that I could sentence you to be placed in the custody of the State of Idaho and sent to St. Anthony? (St. Anthony's being the equivalent of California's CYA or California Youth Authority) My response: (I believe it was something like) Well, if you think you can do that then let's see you do it, 'cause that's where I'm gonna end up anyway! Now whose blood was boiling? Well it must have been his because that's exactly what he did with

103
103

me. FUCK 'EM! I was ready! Besides, I was curious…I had heard a lot about this place. It's the same place Rose had been sent to years before, so I had been hearing about it for a long time. Though Rose had had long since been released, I figured it was my turn.

19

Transport to this institution was a bitch! First of all, it was on the other side of the state in eastern Idaho near W. Yellowstone Park. Myself and 3 other hardened criminals were handcuffed for the entire ride and driven by two asshole marshals, who ate McDonalds while we were fed sack lunches, in one of those County issued vans. I don't think I ever said, "Fuck you!" so many times in one car ride in my whole life more than on that ride. As a result, I had these guys pretty agitated and by the time we finally got there, they were more than happy to be rid of the little bastard in the back seat.

Let me set this up for ya. At the time of my arrival, St. Anthony's consisted of 5 complete cottages and one that was under construction, making a total of 6. Five are all male, one is for females. There is an administration building, a medical/intake building, two gymnasiums (the old and the new), an academic building where the school is located, as well as canteen (commissary), and a cafeteria-style chow hall, which is connected to the new gym. The place is completely self-contained with its own laundry facility and dairy, only lacking its own slaughterhouse. It even has its own powerhouse. There are no fences, however there is an armed security patrol of one guard, 24 hours a day, 7 days a week. In the event of an escape attempt the security unit is equipped with a radio that shares the same frequency as the radios that each staff member on shift is required to carry, including any and all surrounding local law enforcement agencies.

Each cottage is named after a mountain range. Intake/Medical is named Wausatch; the girls cottage is Teton; Targhee is for the kids from 10 to 14; Caribou houses kids from 15 to 17; Sawtooth is a cottage for kids with mental disorders, suicidal etc.; Bitterroot is intended for returnees and the oldest kids; and Yellowstone, which was still under construction at the time of my arrival, would later be referred to as the Behavioral Unit or BU. Now upon arrival at St. Anthony, each kid is immediately stripped of any and all street clothing and given a physical examination. The clothing is then sent to laundry to be washed and tagged with the individual's name. The new resident is then issued a one piece red (bright red) jumpsuit, commonly referred to as a "Zoot suit" and is required to wear it for the first 30 days of residency, after which time you are allowed your own clothes.

The cottage I'm admitted into is Targhee. In the entrance is a large foyer with long wardrobe style coat racks on each side filled with the jackets of the some 100 inhabitants. Shoes are not allowed inside and are therefore are piled all below the jackets. I am instructed by my escort (security) to hang my State issued jacket and take my shoes off, at which time the on duty staff greets us. Now this guy is a character, his name is Mr. M or Mr. Mic. Remember that sitcom called "One day at a Time?" Now remember the guy who played "Schneider?" Now picture that guy with an ill proportioned fat ass, a big radio, a huge set of keys hanging from his side, and BAM! you've got Mr. Mic. My first thought, after laying eyes on this guy, was what fun it was going to be learning his idiosyncrasies well enough to imitate him. Mr. Mic was a chain smoker and he often punctuated himself by taking one long exaggerated drag from his cigarette, squinting his eyes and then either dramatically crushing it out into the ashtray or cocking his arm back, pausing and then dramatically over exaggerating flicking the butt into the ground, always accompanied with some bazaar never before seen facial contortion. He had one of those ear piercing nasally voices and he knew exactly how and when to apply it. As I enter the cottage the foyer leads to a hallway and the first room to the left is the staff office, a small cubical type room with squared windowless steel panes all the way around it. Beyond it is the main dayroom and it is a pretty good-sized room, big enough to accommodate about 3 couches, a ping-pong table and a pool table. I notice about 80 kids in this room, watching T.V., playing pool, whatever have ya! Mr. Mic takes me into the office, tells me to have a seat and sits down himself, kicking his feet up on the desk and lighting up a cigarette. I'm thinking, this guy has gotta know how ridiculous he looks, but the great thing about Mr. Mic is that he really doesn't give a shit and I like that. I figure anybody who can go around looking' and acting like this guy and not give a shit what anyone thinks has got balls. So here I am, in my little red jumpsuit sitting across from this chain smoking Schneider/ Chris Farley type guy, and he starts in with the speech. "I'm gonna tell ya right now, Mr. Snowball, I don't tolerate any shit out of any of you little fuckers. If you think you're

107

gonna come in here, start dinkin' around and fuck with my program, well you're in for a world of hurt, 'cause now that you're here, your ass is mine! Bedtime is at nine and when you go out there you're to keep your hands to yourself!" "Mr. C", he barks...and a kid appears in the doorway, "Show Mr. Snowball here to the dorm area and instruct him on how his bunk is expected to be maintained, show him the chore list and explain to him how we do business around here." "Mr. Snowball", follow Mr. C and listen very closely to what he has to say."

Kelly C was a cool kid. He walked me back to the dorm and as I rolled my eyes, I said, "What a freak!" (referring to Mr. Mic). He said, "Yea, but he's a good guy, his bark is a lot worse than his bite...he just lays it on like that for shock value, but he's really a softy. You ever make a bed with hospital corners?" "Uh, uh", I answered. He proceeded to show me what that meant, how to do it and then walked me back out the hall to show me and explain how the chore list worked. Once that was explained, we walked into the dayroom where we were quickly flocked by a group of curious kids. I was relieved to see that there were a few familiar faces from the Ada County detention center, but most of the kids I didn't know. These were kids from all over the State of Idaho and they all had there own very unique story behind why they were at St. Anthony.

Kelly explained the "program", you know, the pre-requisite for release. He explained that the first 30 days was a probationary observation period, and after that you would graduate to phase one. There were 7 phases in all, four weeks per phase. For example: The successful completion of the first week of phase one would be noted as 1^1, the second week of phase 1 is noted as 1^2 etc., all the way up to 6^4. The last and final phase was referred to as "PR", an abbreviation for pre-release. A successful transition through each phase was dependant upon behavior, the level of participation in group therapy, as well as a kid's willingness to encourage a positive influence on peers. Written reports kept track of disruptive behavior with special little titles like "defiance", "vulgar and abusive", and "GMD" (Group Management disturbance), my personal favorite. Disciplinary action consisted of "standing wall", "sitting chair", and of course, my personal favorite, "isolation" or solitary confinement.

Let's start with the description of what standing wall meant. You point your toes in toward the baseboard of a wall, put your hands behind your back and place your nose on the wall. If at any time your nose leaves the wall, your time starts over. Time could be allocated according to the discretion of the staff member who put you there, which meant it could be as long as they want... unless, of course, you were Randy Snowball, who had a gift for receiving so many disciplinary reports of every kind all at once. In that case, you could be scheduled to stand wall either beginning at 3:30 lasting until bedtime or all day restriction that began at 7:30am and ended at bedtime with a bathroom break once an hour and a 5-minute shower (strictly enforced), at a time that was convenient to the staff on duty.   Sitting chair was of the same venue where timelines were concerned, except that you were restricted to sitting in the hallway in a wooden chair "on silence" (no talking), with your hands at your sides, with the same set of rules and the same breaks. If you were standing wall you were permitted to sit in a chair in the hall but only for as long as the time required to finish your meal. A maximum of 30 minutes was allowed. The reason for my having such a detailed and accurate account of the disciplinary structure at St. Anthony is, of course, not a result of Kelly C sitting me down and describing it all in depth, but rather because I experienced it first hand.

20

The first rule I broke was vulgar and abusive language and it was toward the end of the shift for a staff member named Kurt H. He heard me cursing from the office and came out barking, "SNOWBALL, HIT THE WALL!" I spun around and responded with, "FUCK YOU, MOTHER FUCKER!" Oops! Now let me tell you a little about Kurt H. First of all the guy is a cop in the real world and not only that but he's a black belt and as if that isn't enough, he's a black belt cop with this Nazi Socialist SS officer disposition. You know the type that gets red in the face when their authority is challenged? Well, this guy snatched me up by the hair like a rag doll, takes me out into the hall and shoves my nose into the wall and then goes to walk away. As soon as his back is turned and he's far enough away, I pick up the nearest wooden chair and go to bash his head in with it. But hey, come on, I'm 13 and this guy is an SS officer with the National Socialist Party or at least a black belt cop with a power trip. Anyway, so what's the difference? I was quickly disarmed and found my face and nose being reacquainted with the cinder block wall. He informed me that he had no problem holding me there for the next hour until the end of his shift and you know what...my loathing defiance made sure he did. This was the beginning of a deep seeded mutually hateful relationship that would last until the day of my release. From that day on, I made an absolute point, at any cost, to make Mr. H's shift a living hell. I manipulated him by being compliant at times, gaining his trust to the point that he would begin to believe that his methods were the sole reason for my seemingly compliant and submissive attitude adjustment and then "BAM" I would cause a group management disturbance (GMD). It was always the same trap I used for Mr. H. I would simply do something that would cause him to have to come out of the office and regulate...you know...like get up and turn the channel on the TV during the middle of a movie or stage a verbal disagreement with someone...it never failed. Since he was the type of person who was poised and eager to impose his authority, I played on that. My campaign with Mr. H was to expose his tendency to respond to my challenges with over reactive abusive aggression, and it worked. It took a lot of standing wall and a lot of defiant resistance, along with the one thing he just hated to hear, which was "FUCK YOU, MOTHER FUCKER!" But finally, he began to get reprimanded by his superiors. Our little war lasted so long that somebody decided to take a closer look at the situation and apparently, after some observation, didn't like what they saw. But the problem only revealed itself as a result of H's coming up against a kid who wasn't afraid of standing wall or chair or solitary confinement or even him. This is something that he hadn't considered since all the kids before me had quickly complied in fear of his hostile and aggressive methods. He was praised for quick results and his capacity for hostility had always gone unnoticed. Who would dare take the brunt of it long enough for it to reveal itself? The first indication of progress in my

112

campaign against Mr. H was the slow and gradual decay of mutual respect between he and other staff members. I knew something was going sour for him when he would clock out at the end of his shift and leave me standing wall, instructing the next staff member clocking in that I was to remain there, standing wall, until bedtime. Well what started happening was that as soon as he was out the door, the new guy would say, "Snowball, go watch TV." It was especially funny if Mr. Mic was clockin' in because then I would get to listen to Mr. Mic blatantly undermine H's wishes to his face. Oh yeah! It was well worth getting in trouble a couple of hours before shift change, being placed on the wall and waiting for Mr. Mic. I would take extra steps to rile Mr. H up just before 4:00 o'clock. That way I could bait him into thinking he could impose his supreme authority on me even after he'd gone home. It never failed. I would spread it out to maybe once or twice a week because even though Mr. H was oblivious, most of the time, to my antagonizing his temperament, Mr. Mic knew exactly what I was doing. It went without saying that the only reason he participated was because he didn't approve of H's methods long before I came along and he respected me for taking the brunt of it long enough for Mr. H to expose himself as the asshole he really was. He was obviously in no position to do this himself, plus he really enjoyed this new opportunity I had created for him to tell Mr. H to go "fuck" himself. As far as Mr. Mic was concerned, after 4:00 o'clock these kids were his and nobody was going to be imposing their authority on "his" shift. So when the clock struck 4 it was, "Snowball, go watch TV", no matter what Mr. H said…and "yes" I enjoyed myself immensely on the day Kurt H had transferred himself to Caribou. It took 3 months of outright antagonistic defiant behavior and my efforts succeeded in ridding myself of a man I deeply loathed. That's not all my behavior succeeded in doing, it also succeeded in getting me heavily medicated. When it was all said and done after that three-month war, somebody decided I needed 300 milligrams of Lithium 4 times a day along with 100 milligrams of Tofrinil and 50 milligrams of Elevil, 3 times a day. Oh yeah, things got real mellow, real fast for Randy Snowball.

I was scheduled for one hour per week with the prescribing psychiatrist and once again asked to take a battery of tests. Somebody was interested in my IQ. They were able to learn nothing from the tests since a psychological profile is easily manipulated and concealed on paper and all they had left for behavioral observation was an extremely sedated subject, so that's what they settled for. Things were actually pretty smooth sailing for a while. I got to go to the chow hall and lay eyes on other kids from other cottages including the girls, something I hadn't done since my arrival. Through this exposure to the mainstream agenda and the small talk among peers, I discovered that I was already quite well known. Once again my name had preceded me. Since I had been on restriction from day one and it had taken so long just to be permitted to eat in the chow hall, this in itself resulted in there being a mystique that surrounded my name as well as my character. There was a lot of talk yet no one really knew who I was, my not having been exposed to this new arena for any length of time as yet. People were very curious and so was I.

I found out from a kid named Shane that there was a way to get close to the chicks by going to church on Sunday. He also mentioned that the Reverend had a piano and would probably let me play it sometimes. My eyes lit up when I heard chicks and piano in the same sentence. Instantly I knew what I must do. **Repent!..** and on the following Sunday…there I was… ordered up…two by two…in the church line…marching to Sunday Services. Halleluiah! Church for all of the male cottages was the perfect place to flirt with the girls from the girls' dorm as well as pass notes. It was like a room full of male and female dogs, sniffin' each other's asses…but I had other plans; I was going to play that piano. My plan was to buddy up to Reverend Fred and convince the cottage staff that it would be therapeutic for me to come in on the weekdays for an hour a day so I could play. Well on that first day at church my plans came together even better than I could have dreamed. Not only was I able to convince the cottage staff of the therapeutic qualities of this idea but Reverend Fred was happy to allow it and in fact he didn't mind letting me play for everyone after the service.

On that day a star was born and everyone on campus was introduced to Randy Snowball. I didn't just sing some song; I sang a song that I made up as I went along about everyone in the room. People were shocked when they suddenly realized my subtle and sometimes not so subtle references to them or their character. FUN STUFF! I played until Reverend Fred became visually uncomfortable with the idea that I might be getting more attention than God. Reverend Fred was cool and he was a religious fanatic. He didn't want anyone losing sight of why we had all gathered there that day and it wasn't so that Randy Snowball could entertain us all. It was to praise the Lord! Halleluiah! and I had to give him that. Not that I had a choice when he asked me to stop, but what I mean to say is that I graciously excused myself grateful for the unexpected opportunity to perform. Even though he knew that most of us were there to flirt, he was always pleased to see that so many of us would show up in the house of God to hear him preach the Gospel because it made him feel good to preach to a full house... whatever their reasons for being there. He allowed me to play after services on one or two more occasions, but no more after that. You didn't have to be a brainiac to see that I was playing for the sole purpose of furthering my popularity, though he was cool enough to allow me to come in 3 times a week for an hour and play by myself alone in the Chapel. I would give anything for a recording of those sessions. As you may imagine this was a time of great musical and spiritual evolution in my life. The fact that it took place in a chapel was eerily ironic. I became fantastically popular in what seemed an instant.

At St. Anthony, I was not only well liked by my peers, but also by most staff members. I quickly began to experience the weight of responsibility that is accompanied with what it means to be popular in such a small community of faces that never change. Oh sure, I was likable, but I was far from having the kind of wisdom and patience that is required for handling that scale of popularity on the long-term frontier of constant dissection. Those kinds of tools only come from mileage and that was one area I had zero mileage in...but I enjoyed that popularity until it became a pain in my ass. I was great at marketing myself, but I was bad at gracefully bowing out when I got sick of it. One thing I hadn't givin' any thought to was that I had to live on this stage along with my fans, 24 hours a day, 7 days a week. I was always expected, not only by others but also by myself, to respond to certain things a certain way. I was constantly being asked my opinion in things I knew nothing about and had no interest in knowing anything about. Being asked to settle disputes I had nothing to do with. Being asked to write the lyrics to songs, poems and love letters for somebody to send to their girlfriend. It's hard to bow out when there is nowhere to bow out too. I began to feel a bit invaded and disliked the fact that I had caused this situation myself. I felt stupid for making myself into an image that I felt was overwhelming me. But it all happened so fast: the name; the music; the quick wit...it was a demanding role to play, particularly when the demand is constant. I had to find some way to get some peace and what better way than to break some rules.

I was in luck because right at about that time Mr. H's replacement started his training. His name was Mr. W and he was one of those "by the book" guys who liked to make it known that he didn't mind writing reports. I mean this guy would write a kid up for even the most ridiculous rule violations. He immediately honed in on me, because by the time he started I was no doubt extremely comfortable and had become accustomed to getting away with murder. The difference between Mr. W and Mr. H was that for one thing Mr. W wouldn't physically force a kid into compliance. If I refused to stand wall or defied his requests, he would simply escort me to solitary confinement. I decided that if he was going to write me up for every little thing then I had no choice but to break every little rule and that included every big rule too. In one night I racked up enough disciplinary reports to net me the next 8 months in solitary confinement. I wanted peace of mind and I got it. I accomplished this by saying the most disgusting things I could think of about his wife and family. I'm not going to repeat any of it here. I stayed in the solitary confinement cell in Targhee for about the first 3 months, but then somebody decided move me to Caribou lockdown, probably because they got tired of hearing the obscenities I would yell at Mr. W from under the door every time he'd pass by my cell. The difference between the two places was immense. While Targhee, Bitterroot, and Teton were all built in the 50's, Caribou, Sawtooth, Laundry and the powerhouse buildings were all established sometime around 1910. You can't imagine what this cell was like. Have you ever smelled an old fan motor from the 30's or 40's when it burns up? Or the dust from an old Kirby vacuum? Or walked into an elderly persons home whose furniture, carpet and even the television have remained the same for 50 years? Well add another 20 to that 50 and you've just walked into a time machine complete with the odor from an era long since forgotten... "Caribou lockdown." Caribou was a two-story building and the two solitary confinement cells were upstairs across the hall from each other. They were 8 by 12 cells with two bunks (bunk bed style) with your standard all in one jailhouse sink & toilet set-up. I suppose that at one time the floors had linoleum on them but it had long since been worn down to where it was completely black everywhere. The one window was a thick clear plastic one that could be opened by pulling the top outward and pushing the bottom in and up. The window opening itself was paned with thick steel small rectangles. The heater in those cells was one of those thick cast iron radiator looking monstrosities that made really loud ticking sounds when it warmed up. The place had to have been painted sometime, but there wasn't one square inch of wall space where somebody hadn't scratched his or her name and date or just something. The oldest date I found in that cell was 1932. Now the rules at Caribou lockup were a bit different from the rules at Targhee. At Targhee I could read stuff like

Readers Digest and magazines, but at Caribou the only reading allowed was the Bible. Since this was a dorm for older kids, the treatment was, to say the least, a little different by staff. If you yelled any shit from under the door or out the window they would simply come up and put tape on your mouth and then handcuff your arms and legs to the four corners of the bunk and leave you there for about 6 hours. If you think I'm bullshitting I'm sure you can find out for yourself by checking the list of things the staff were eventually prosecuted for doing years later. I don't have to check, I had it done to me once and watched them do it to many others in that cell, among other things. At times I did have a couple of cellmates, but they were short timers. Nobody had as much time in solitary as I did.

Now the dude across the hall in the other cell was close, but I had him beat by about two weeks. His name was Willy. I had heard of him because he was in the same club of the top 5 non-compliant kids in the institution that I was, but I had never met the guy, up to that point. Aside from the occasional head nods we would exchange through the barely translucent, scratched to hell, tiny rectangle plastic window on the door, I didn't know him because even then all I could see was a blurry image. That changed one night thanks to a kid named Shane. I got up from a nap for one of the few highlights of my day, which was watching the cottage order up... two by two... outside just before the march to chow hall. They would line up 3 times a day, before every meal and be counted by name like role call. I would watch them leave from my window and would watch them return, playfully flipping off everyone who looked up. No hard feelings...it's just something I did in a desperate attempt for acknowledgement. Everything was pretty "ho-hum" that day as I watched them return from chow. They had all stopped in the front of the cottage waiting for Mr. M to open the door. Now let me tell you a little something about Mr. M. You ever see one of those leather bound photo albums with pictures of cattle ranchers, miners and outlaws from the old west? Well Mr. M was in there. He was the guy with the huge back that looked more like a piece of real-estate, a great big bushy handlebar moustache with the classic sleepy eyes, long face and big floppy assed jowls. You know, like a giant Wilfred Brimley...and if you don't know who Wilfred Brimley is then...FUCK YOU!

Anyway, as Mr. M unlocks the door, I'm flipping off the usual people in line when I notice somebody break from the rear of the line and start running toward the open field. Mr. M sees him and is in hot pursuit. It's Shane and he's running. He's got a short fence to hop and he does it so successfully but Mr. M is right on his ass. Just as they're both over the fence, ole Shane takes a couple of steps forward and slips on a rock, but as he's going down...with Mr. M right behind him...he takes a swing (oops)...he misses, but Mr. M, on the other hand, (no pun intended) lands his own hard right to the jaw of Shane ...lays him out and puts him on a soft diet for the next month. You ever try to eat with a busted jaw? You can't! Poor Fucker! But any sympathy I may have felt for him at that moment died when I heard the lock on my cell door go "click", the door opened and in walked Shane.

21

Now let me tell ya, the first 30 days with my new cellmate wasn't so bad because his jaw was wired shut and I got most of his food, but as soon as that wire came out, shit, I almost re-broke his jaw myself on several occasions just to shut him up. I don't know what the guy's problem was but he just wouldn't shut the fuck up! Not only that, he would bang his head against the door every time someone walked by outside the door. Finally staff came in one night and put him in these leather restraints that bound him to the lower bunk. It took him about an hour but he chewed through them and freed himself. The same night they came in and put him in a strait jacket. That fucker begged me for hours saying, "come on Snowball, just one strap, just loosen this one strap and I won't bug you anymore." My answer, "fuck you and shut the fuck up!" I liked watching this guy suffer because before he came along I had my own little peaceful cell. Now I had staff coming in there all the time searching and fucking with my world. Every once in a while that night, I would yell out, "squirm mother fucker squirm." That's exactly what he did for the next 4 hours until he had somehow squirmed himself completely free from the strait jacket. All I know is that I was almost asleep when I heard that heavy canvas hit the floor. When staff came to check on him they opened the door and immediately blamed me for helping him. I was pissed! I responded to their allegations with "fuck you!" "I don't even like this stupid fucker…why would I help him?" But to no avail, they were so convinced I had helped him they gave me an additional 14 days and then moved me across the hall into a cell with the guy I only knew as a blurry image, that I would head nod to once in a while, Willie.

Willie was the other guy on campus who had made a name for himself by his refusal to comply and notorious defiant behavior, but he was older. Now...you would think that a guy who is defiant toward staff would have an attitude problem, but not so in the case of Willie. Willie, in my best description, was kind of like Paul Newman, cast in the role of Cool Hand Luke. He was tall, lanky, well built, a good-looking dude and the best thing, he loved to hear me sing. We spent 5 months in that little run down cell laughin' and singin' and jokin', playin' basketball with a cup and little paper balls, all the way up to the day Willie's time in lockdown was up and we shook each others hands and hugged goodbye. However it wasn't the last I would see of him. Two weeks later I was released from lockdown and transferred back to Targhee. Even though my mode had shifted from defiant to sneaky, I still ended up back in Targhee solitary for two more months. It was during that time I got to watch the grand opening of the BU or Behavioral Unit. They called it Yellowstone and it was right across from my cell on the other side of the tennis courts. The tennis courts were connected to it through a fenced-in walkway that led to its back door. Everyday at 2:00 o'clock the 40 kids that lived there would run out through the back door, one by one, down the caged in walkway to their assigned positions and yell out, their number and, "arrived sir!" One by one, until all 40 of them had come out and were standing in their assigned positions at which time the guard would come along and un-cuff them, one by one. They would then start their calisthenics. It was a boot camp for kids. The only thing I can think of that kept me from becoming a resident at Yellowstone was age. The last two months of solitary in Targhee were enough and I never went back. I submitted…only to play the game and eventually became pretty good at it.

I discovered that there was a cool social scene at St. Anthony that I had been missing out on: school, girls, playing Frisbee, and baseball games against other cottages! St. Anthony even had it's own basketball team that would play against teams from surrounding communities in the new gym. The new gymnasium had a full sized basketball court complete with pull out bleachers and a professional electronic scoreboard. Those games were a blast. The entire campus would attend so there was a lot of flirting and note passing with the girls. But the place was charged with excitement. There was one player on our team that could really play some basketball and always got the crowd worked up! His name was Wilson. Now this kid couldn't have been more than 5 feet tall but man he could really shoot and move. He was one of those kinds of guys that would bring us all the way from behind for the win. He had a modest personable disposition, a good sense of humor and man could he shoot some hoop. I wonder whatever happened to ole Wilson…hmmm.

Anyway, I eventually began to work my way through the program. I attended the on campus school every day and I had good days and bad days, but I went...begrudgedly doing whatever it took to complete each phase until finally, almost a year and a half later, I made pre-release status. Two days before I was to be released, I started hearing the name of a new girl who had just arrived at St. Anthony. Along with the name came a whole bunch of hype about how pretty she was. Her name was (is) Sheila and I got my chance to see what all the hype was, in passing, at the chow hall. Yeah, she was pretty but to tell you the truth, I was so caught up with the idea of getting released in 48 hours that I really didn't give her the time of day. Had I done so, I may have wanted to stay. Two days later I was released and driven to the Greyhound bus depot where I caught the next bus to Boise.

22

When I arrived in Boise, I was met by Dorothy, who picked me up and drove the next 20 or so miles to the new family home in a town just outside of Boise called Nampa. As we came to the city of Nampa and she kept driving, I had to ask, "Where the hell is this place?" "Just a little further" she would say. Just a little further my ass! This place was out in the middle of nowhere. Surrounded by beet fields and a bird refuge, two miles from the nearest store, nonetheless, this was a nice place. Set on over two acres of land, a 5-bedroom house with the classic style, four white pillars in front, with a three-car garage and overlooking the valley from atop a small hill, it was nothing to whine about, though I'm sure I did anyway. I know I was pissed about having to live in Nampa because all of my friends lived in Boise. Nothing a little hitchhiking couldn't fix. In the meantime, I was enrolled in West Junior High, but I didn't last very long there. I was expelled for absences after a couple of months. I was still on probation with Glenn E as my probation officer.

And one day ole Glenn came out to pick me up...he and his marshal buddy. We use to call him "McLeod" at the Ada County Detention Center, but his name was (is) Marshall Mike T. Marshall Mike was waiting outside in one of those (at the time) standard issue Plymouth Satellites while Glenn just sorta let himself in the front door. I was shocked to see him when I opened the door considering it was a school day and I wasn't in school. I knew he'd learned of my expulsion and was there to take me in...but he's playin' it off with small talk. What he doesn't know is that my bedroom has it's own outside door that leads to a ground level patio. So while he's talking I'm nodding my head in agreement, yeah, yeah, uh huh...sure thing Glenn. Slowly inching my way closer and closer to that doorknob and then, "BAM!" The next thing ya know I'm "goose stepping" in a full-blown sprint down an irrigation road that ran along side the beet field behind our house. Ole Glenn's in hot pursuit but then; "oh shit" here comes the Plymouth, right behind me and closing fast. Well, I've got to get off that road or he's gonna run me over, I'm thinking. So I goose step-it into the beet field and no sooner than I do that, when ole Marshall Mike pulls right up next to me, still on the road but keepin' pace with me. Of-course, Glenn's still behind me and gaining fast when I notice the windows are down in the Plymouth and I hear this bastard laughin at me, "ha ha ha ha ha". I couldn't help it, I started laughin' too...and as a result I lost my breath and collapsed in the dirt, trying to catch my breath and laugh at the same time. I mean, where the hell did I think I was gonna go? Glenn had caught up by then...he's got the cuffs out and he's saying to me, "not bad for an old guy, huh?" And all the way back to Boise I'm carrying on about how I could have lost 'em had it not been for that meddling marshal, of course, they're both sitting in the front seat nodding their heads, chuckling saying, "surrrrre Snowball." I don't know how long I got in detention that time, but it wasn't very long. When I did get out, my case was transferred to Nampa and I was enrolled in a new school, South Junior High.

South was only 2 miles straight down the road from our house. I didn't know anyone there, but everyone seemed to know me. Besides being the new kid from St. Anthony, I guess you could say, I stuck out like a sore thumb. Being the only *longhair* in a school full of kids from the surrounding farming community, it was easy to stick out. And if that weren't enough, I use to take a General Electric boom box along with me to school that would blare "AC/CD" from the lunchroom everyday. Hey, you could do that at this school. Sure there was a couple of times I was asked to turn it down and when that happened I would pick up my stereo, turn it up, put it on my shoulder and walk out the two front doors of the school to begin my two mile walk home...radio blaring, Highway to Hell! The principal, Mr. A, was a very cool dude. After a while it became routine to wait until Dorothy was out of sight, after dropping me off for school, and then turn right around and simply walk home. I would be walking along and suddenly this little truck would pull up next to me. I would look to see who it was and it would be Mr. A. He would lean over and open the passenger side door and say, "ya want a ride?" You can understand my apprehension, but I took the gamble...I hopped in and sure enough he gave me a ride home. On the way he explained that there was no point in forcing me to be somewhere I didn't want to be. Back in the days when I would actually stick it out for the day,

Mr. A was in charge of giving me my Lithium at lunchtime. Everyday I would go into his office, close the door and out of his desk drawer he would take out my bottle of pills and his pint of whiskey and say, "alright now, you take your medicine and I'll take mine...on three....1, 2, 3...and we would simultaneously swallow our medication. His just happened to be a shot of whiskey. So we had already established some degree of trust long before the rides home.

Before the end of that school year, there was to be a talent show. Yeeee, Haw!!! I wouldn't miss it for the world, especially since I was a lot better at playing the piano since my grade school performance. So, of-course, I signed up and when the time came, the gymnasium was packed, about 800 people. If I was nervous, it didn't show. I hadn't rehearsed anything and I had no idea what I was gonna play. I just made believe I was at home, as if I were walking by the piano and decided to play. Though I don't remember the words to the song I played, I do remember the "kind" of song it was. It was an ad-libbed anti-establishment song that everyone could easily relate to, and apparently everyone did because I got another standing ovation for it. I walked home after the show feeling like a million bucks. Yea...I walked...at that age and even now, I have a hard time excepting compliments, but it isn't just the compliments...it's really more the questions. How long have I been playing? Did I write the song? How did I learn to sing like that? Just a constant repetitive battery of questions. My motto: Perform and get the hell out of there! Weird, some might even say *rude* and to that I would say, "yes". But though I agree, it doesn't lessen my desire to leave by one iota. I managed somehow to finish that school year out without winding up in detention, but once school was out, I grabbed my skateboard and I was hitchhiking to Boise to hang out at Tom R's.

Since Dorothy still worked in Boise, I could always catch a ride home whenever I was ready to come home. Tom and I would get drunk at his little place and listen to Pink Floyd's "The Wall", singing every word together, but then I would always get antsy and want to go downtown to the Cruz. Tom would always want to stay home and that was cool because it meant I had a place nearby to bring a chick...if I happened to pick one up. It was on one of these drunken antsy nights, while walking the Cruz, that I would meet a guy named Jim W. I was walking along, singing my ass off, as I often did, and as I made my way oblivious to anything but the sound of my voice, this guy suddenly approached me with a Wink Martindale twinkle in his eye. His exact words were, "hey that sounds really good, do you sing with any bands here in town?" I said, "no", I just sing! "Well dude would ya like to, 'cause I've never heard anyone sing like that around here. Why don't you come to our practice tomorrow, look here's my number; call me tomorrow and I'll come pick you up where ever you are. You can check it out; see what you think." All of this before he even asked my name. We exchanged names and numbers, shook hands and I went on my way. By the time the next day rolled around I had completely forgotten about the phone number written on a matchbook cover in my jacket pocket with the name "Jim" written next to it. But, at around 3:00 o'clock the following day, I received a call that wiped out any thoughts I may have had about how serious this guy was. Dinga linga ling...Me: "Hello" Jim: "Hey, is this Randy?" "Yeah, who's this?" "It's Jim" "Jim who?" "Jim W...I met you last night downtown. I talked to you about singing for a rock and roll band...now where ya at? I'm coming to pick you up!" Now, how the hell do you say "no" to a guy like that? You don't! I found myself obediently giving my address and directions to my house and a half an hour later I found myself sitting in the passenger seat of Jim's candy apple GTO on my way to my first band practice.

Now these guys were a hoot. We practiced for hours that day. The beauty of it was...that I had the lyrics to just about every classic rock and roll song already memorized...so it was just a process of determining which songs I was comfortable singing, what the band was capable of playing, how many songs we all knew in total and which songs we all wanted to play but hadn't learned as yet. Oh yeah, and discipline. What I mean by that is quite simply getting everyone to stop dinkin' around on their instruments long enough to allow the required discussion it takes to get anything done. It sounds elementary doesn't it? Well, from the view of a lead singer...it's anything but! One of the things you have to consider (I would learn the hard way) is that really good lead singers are very hard to find. It is because of this that many bands wind-up playing instrumentally through a song list for a long time before a vocalist comes along. Unfortunately, a band can become very uncompromising to even the most practical needs of a new lead singer. For example: Bands that have been playing for a long time without a lead singer have a great tendency to play very loud. Why, because they don't have to concern themselves with a singer or an audience trying to hear the words of a song over the band. With no singer they become accustomed to playing the music as loud as they want. In most cases you're dealing with some huge egos and with that in mind, let me tell you, the last thing an up and coming garage band is going to want to do is listen to some seemingly cocky new lead singer who doesn't even own his own microphone. Or have him come in and start dictating the mechanical rapport of a band that played well up until he came along. It is for this very reason that many potentially great garage bands remain just that, "Garage Bands." On the other side of the coin there are a lot of singers out there that make it increasingly difficult for good vocalists in search of professionalism by imposing unreasonable and impractical requirements. These megalomaniacs only make it more difficult for a lot of really, really good musicians to break through the ego barrier.

I have seen how a few bad experiences with lead singers can make a perfectly good band become well, shall we say, less receptive to constructive criticisms. In my case, I had two advantages. Number 1; I wasn't a so-so singer, I was an excellent singer; and #2 Jim W, having been playing in bands for years before I could even wipe my own ass, could see that I was a very green, very moldable excellent singer, so he wasn't about to allow a show of unprofessionalism by the other members frustrate me into not wanting to sing for the band.

23

Blah, Blah, Blah and Bam! I'm the lead singer in my first Rock-N-Roll Band. The name? Crystal Image. For a while all we did was practice, practice, practice..., which was more than enough fun for me. I had never had so much fun playing and bonding with a group of friends in my life. Never mind the bottle of whiskey Jim always had on hand as an added incentive. We would have band practice for a couple of hours and by the time we were done I'd be all sweaty from literally just singing my ass off...ears ringing from the amplifiers and drunk as a skunk from straight shots of whiskey. If it happened to be a Friday night, I would usually have Jim drop me off at the Cruz.

One night, after being dropped off on a unusually crowded Friday night, I began to make my way down the sidewalk saying "hello" to various acquaintances until I happened upon a character I considered to be a very good friend. His name was (is) Jim K. I had never known Jim K outside of the time we spent incarcerated in St. Anthony. From the moment we laid eyes on one another we were overjoyed; not unlike two former POW's recognizing each other on the street. We hugged and laughed and when the initial shock wore down Jim looked at me and said, "Hey ya know Willie W is down the street at Wizards Arcade with Sheila R playing Asteroids." "Willie W"...I responded in shock! I don't know why, but for some reason I just never thought I would see that guy again. Jim said, "lets go." We walked into Wizards, and I'll be damned but standing there in the flesh playing Asteroids was my old cellmate from solitary confinement...Willie W...aka...Cool Hand Luke! Standing directly behind him, waiting impatiently and rolling her eyes as Jim and I approached, was Sheila R. I had my finger up to my mouth as if to say, "shhhhh." I stood there beside Sheila until he was done playing. Which wasn't easy because on a scale of 1 to 10, (where Sheila was concerned) she was an 11. It struck me odd that Willie would be playing Asteroids, because to tell you the truth, Sheila really didn't strike me as the type that would tolerate that kind of neglect from anyone, specifically a boyfriend. Tall, skinny with strawberry blonde hair that hung to the middle of her back and a smile to die for, she could have been with anyone she wanted, and yet here she was standing behind this guy playing Asteroids at Wizards. All I could do was smile, roll my eyes back at her and when she looked away I gave her a quick once over and shook my head in confusion...but I know she saw me in her peripheral vision. I know a smirk when I see one. It really didn't matter because quite frankly she could have been a "12" and there's still no way I would have jeopardized this reunion with my old friend Willie. When he finally did turn around, Sheila and I were in a long deep French kiss and had to be pulled apart..............NOT! *(Come on, have a sense of humor Sheila...hardy, har har. I just couldn't resist, since we both know that's not what happened. What better place to* "rib" ya? ☺ I'll strike it from the final print, I promise, now back to reality) I lied.

When he finally did turn around, it was as one might expect, a lot of joy and happiness with a big hug. As the four of us walked out of Wizards, Willie and I took the lead and began to talk about old times. I, of course, told him about the band, sang some of the old favorite songs that I use to sing in our cell as we walked along, but there was something different about Willie, and on top of that, I was puzzled as to why we had been walking and talking with Sheila and Jim walking at some distance behind us. That whole night Willie seemed, to put it mildly, preoccupied. On more than one occasion Sheila had made no bones about checking me out, not with spoken words but with a glance every once in a while.

At some point in the evening, the four of us managed to meet up with another St. Anthony acquaintance. His name was Calvin A and he said he had a place we could all go and kick back. He said he was renting it, but I had a hard time buying this story because it looked uninhabited and abandoned from the inside out. The lights were on so what the hell, we were all tired from walking around most of the night. It was too late to buy any alcohol, but it was nearing 6:00 am at which time the sale of alcohol would resume. What's funny is that the only ones with any money were Sheila and myself. I had 6 bucks and she had 10. We both dutifully handed over our cash and when it came to be about 6 o'clock, Calvin and Willie headed off to the store, leaving myself, Sheila and Jim waiting in this weird house for their return, and waiting, and waiting, and waiting until finally I just had to get the hell out of there. I believe Jim was asleep on the floor when I left but Sheila was lying down on a couch opposite from me. We had both laid down on separate couches across from each other wide awake just eyeballing the shit out of each other, which, of course, is why I had to get the hell out of there. I just couldn't take it anymore and she knew it. Like I said, I know a smirk when I see one. I headed over to Tom's house and waited for Dorothy to get off from work so I could catch a ride home back to Nampa.

It would be a while before I made it back into Boise. My little adventures in Boise were usually 3 and 4 days, sometimes even a week that I would spend bouncing around from friend's house to friend's house, from party to party until I was wiped out and starving. Between that and the 26 miles I would hitchhike whenever I couldn't find a ride to Boise, which was more often than not, it took it's toll and sometimes I would actually hang out at home for a couple of weeks. It wasn't always practical to hitch a ride to Boise and strand myself, so I found myself hanging around at Nampa's little Cruz section of town, 12th Avenue. The main hangout on this popular little stretch was an arcade named, "Spunkies."

A friend of my brother Dan named Randy R had a shit load of mail order speed called "Christmas Trees" to get rid of and I volunteered my salesmanship skills. Even though I didn't know a soul in that downtown arena I was confident I could get the job done. I was leaning up against a little western style fence in front of "Spunkies" smoking a cigarette when another kid came outside and lit up a cigarette. There was the usual head nod and for what seemed like a long time there wasn't a word spoken as we both leaned back on that little fence smoking our cigarettes. Finally real cool like, without looking over and still gazing out into traffic, the kid takes a long drag off his cigarette, exhales and asks, "how's it going and then flicks his cigarette out into the street." "Pretty good...just hangin' out lookin' for somethin' to do", I answered...and then coolly flicked my cigarette. With that the kid turns to me and says, "Name's Danny D and I know what you mean, there ain't much to do around here." "That's for sure, my name's Snowball, Randy Snowball, glad to meet you" and stuck my hand out. We shook and just by lookin' at this dude I could tell the guy had "potential customer" writtin' all over him. So I wound up for the pitch and let him have it with my best "honest" fastball. I said, actually, I'm out here pushin' pills but I don't know anyone...do you do speed? I could see he enjoyed my point blank approach and with a sly smile he responded by asking, "whatta ya got?" We took a walk to the rear of the building to avoid observation and I'll be dammed if ole Danny didn't clean me out that night...and so began the birth of a beautiful friendship. Dan would quickly become one of the best friends I would ever have the privilege of knowing in a lifetime, even after the "Christmas Trees" ran dry! It was through my friendship with Dan that I would meet and establish the foundations for an entirely new circle of friends from that of the friends I had in Boise. I consider myself extremely lucky to have happened across such a circle of people I will always regard as some of the best friends I could ever have. There were many parties, barbecues, concerts, acid trips, mushroom journeys, and just a lot of damn good times.

When I wasn't partying with Dan and company, I still had band practice in Boise. One night I received a call from Jim explaining that we were getting a new drummer for the band. The drummer we had been using, whose father was also a drummer and had his own band, was about to hit the road, which meant our drummer was drum-less, since the drums he was using for our practice belonged to Pop. Since Jim is a resourceful character, he had already lined up a new drummer without missing a beat (no pun). Meet Toni P...

In meeting Toni (our new drummer), I quickly began introductions to yet another fascinating circle of new friends. We began practicing in Toni's garage and I discovered that I was always welcome to crash there, whenever, and however long I wanted. Toni's household consisted of Toni, his three brothers (all younger) David, Dion, Buckwheat and Toni's Mom, Judy. Remember the movie about bowling called "Kingpin?" Starring Woody Harrelson? Now remember his landlady? Well add a couple of cocktails and "Bam", you've got Judy. No disrespect, she's always been good to me and much like Woody's landlady, she just needed a little love.

Toni and I hit it off like brothers. I think Toni could get along with anyone in the world as easygoing as he always was. His tolerance never ceased to amaze me since his house was chaotic with activity ranging between band practice, bong hits, phone calls, cigarette shortages and Snowball always showin' up out of the blue to stay for a couple of days, not to mentions Toni's room always being the hangout for everyone, friends and family alike. I don't know how he or his Mom ever put up with it. As the regularity of our practice sessions increased, it became apparent that a P.A. would be needed if we ever had any real intention of playing anywhere beyond Toni's garage. And once again, good ole Dorothy obliged by purchasing for me one from Jay's Pawn Shop in exchange for some accounting services or maybe she bought it outright, I can't recall. In any case, she provided one as a show of support for my ongoing musical pursuit.

24

By the summer of 1982, I was 15 years old, singing in a rock 'n roll band and basically doing whatever the hell I wanted, much to Dorothy's dismay and frustration. I did nothing of what she would ask me to do in the way of household chores and, in fact if ever I did lift a finger around the house, I would ask to be paid, and only did so when I needed party money. If Dorothy refused my little suggested contractual agreements for housework in exchange for cash, I would threaten to go out thieving, but more often I would simply badger her at work while simultaneously terrorizing Melissa and Dan until she became subjected to repeated phone calls at work from all of us. Sometimes if I had beaten that technique to death or sensed Dorothy's immunity, I would gage her temperament by a few prodding phone calls to her office. Most of them went something like this: Dorothy: "Hello, this is Dorothy Snowball". Me (in a demonic taunting little voice): "what are you doing?" Dorothy (exasperated): "I'm working Randy, what is it?" Me: "Oh you know." Dorothy: "No Randy, I don't." (long pause) Me (demonic voice): "What are you doing?" Dorothy (brink of hysteria): "COME ON, GOD DAMMIT, I'M TRYING TO WORK!" Me (calmly and demonic) "When are you coming home?" "What time do I always come home Randy?" I would conclude with a quick, "Okay, bye." The example I have just given is the portrait of a successful phone prodding...engineered specifically to provide the answers for 3 questions. Is it gonna do any good to use the time

I have left in the day before she comes home to clean well enough to impress her into giving up some cash so I can go party...and if I did do the work, did it sound like she was in a giving mood? Usually if I employed this method I would do an outstanding job on the house. The better the job, the more desperate I was for the cash. The above portrait of this method is the best-case scenario.

Here's an example of a worst case: Dorothy: "Hello this is Dorothy Snowball". Me (demonic voice) "What are you doing?" Dorothy (exasperated): "I'm working Randy, now what is it?" Me (explosive): "FUCK YOU BITCH! Why do you have to be such a fuckin cunt", CLICK...often smashing the phone and then taking the rest of my rage out on either the family dog, my brother Dan or by smashing a window. If there is one thing that has always infuriated me is that ever constant hint of bitchiness that seemed to emanate from her voice. Don't misunderstand me because I say this with every grain of respect and I will be the first to admit she is entitled to for the years of patience and abuse she has endured at my uncompromising volatile hands, but the bitchiness I am referring to is a personality trait that existed long before I came along. From day one, this was something that would instantly set me off; just her tone could do it. At first it was reaction, but as I became older and more conscience of myself it became a matter of choice to respond to it with volatile hostility. Interestingly the level of my hostility as well as the bitchiness in her tone have experienced some fascinating and sometimes exhaustive spikes of highs and lows on the scale of extremities throughout the course of many years. There were times I would respond with hostility without even being mad at all, but simply because I figured that as long as she was going to respond with that hint of bitchiness in her voice that I so despised, then, of course, I would oblige her with my patented...reaction of a maniac. Though I was well aware of the pressures involved in what it meant to be a single mother of 4 adopted children (as aware as I could have been at age 15), I was still largely the victim of my own emotions and quite often included Dorothy as the primary casualty of my collateral damage. I can only thank God and Dorothy's iron-will that she never made the list of fatalities.

In 1982 I was approached by Dorothy and informed that she had found my natural mother in Southern California. There are no words in existence that can adequately describe the simultaneous flood of emotions I felt at that moment...but if I had to describe the most consuming emotion, I would have to say, "fear." Not only was the single most important question of my life (the question largely responsible for dictating my behavioral evolution) being answered, but I was also being given the opportunity to fly to Los Angeles for the summer and be reunited with not only my mother, but my entire natural family. This included Uncle Bobby, Granny, Aunt Pam, Aunt Julie, Uncle Ronnie...everyone...with the exception of my Grandfather, Jim, whom had since past away. God Bless his soul. This was a terrifying proposition...nonetheless, something I had to do. I found some comfort though, as Dorothy went on to explain, that it would be my decision whether or not to stay in Los Angeles or come back to Idaho, adding that I would always be welcome. My response? "When do I leave?" Any great detailed description of my reaction that day is impossible for me to provide since everything up to the day of my arrival at the LAX airport is a blur. How does one prepare for such an event? It might be interesting to hear what Dorothy's personal account of my behavior during that time may have been, but there's a good chance I may have just stayed away from home all the way up to the day of departure. In any case, for me, it was a blur.

25

I don't even remember saying good-bye at the Boise airport, but when I stepped off the plane at LAX it was an entirely different story. Everything seemed to shift into slow motion as I stepped from the walkway into the waiting area. In that moment, even the audio seemed to slow as I frantically began to search the terminal for faces I desperately wanted to be the first to recognize. This is a bazaar feeling when you consider that I had no pictures of anyone, nothing to stare at during the 10 years of my absence. It would seem that in my desperate attempt to think I could stay close to them, I had convinced myself into believing that I would be the first to have no trouble picking them out in a crowd, specifically Mom. It's almost as if I felt entitled to all the time in the world it might have taken for me to recognize my own mother. After all, they had photos and I didn't, so the least I could get is the benefit of the first recognition…but I didn't stand a chance as I heard, "there he is, there he is, that's him, that's Mark!" Not only did I not make the first identification, but also I had been identified as "Mark", which for a moment threw me from thinking that the voice could be talking about me. But as I searched the crowd, I was able to make a vague positive identification of the smile on the face of a man standing next to my Mother; it was Uncle Bobby 10 years older. He still had that same "Goo Goo Gah Gah" expression in his smile that had been tattooed in my memory from the days of our adventures together, and unbeknownst to me, I hardly needed a photo to remember it.

From the moment I made this recognition everything went from slow motion to warp speed. The next thing I knew I was hugging my Mother, who was crying. As I was hugging her I found myself still studying the only face I really recognized, Uncle Bobby's. At that moment all I really wanted to do was freeze frame everybody but me and Bobby and then have both of us sort of walk out of the scene so I could take a long gander at everyone, Mom, Granny, Julie, my Great Aunt, my new step dad and my new brother, and then turn to Uncle Bobby and ask who every one was and what happened 10 years ago. But life isn't a VCR, is it?

You might think I would have been doing some crying of my own but it was all happening so fast I hardly had any chance to recognize anyone let alone cry over seeing them again. Another thing that caused my indifference was that I had always envisioned sharing the moment along with my sister Marie, you know, together, yeah...together. The whole thing was scaring me and I know my Mother felt my inhibitions because I was involuntarily jerked back and didn't seem to share the overwhelming joy.........I wasn't crying. As I went to each family member one by one hugging them, I could feel my Mother's confusion as she tried to pull herself together, but I wasn't confused. I was overwhelmed and guilty for having experienced the moment without Marie. Not only that, I was trying to figure out how I was to go about asking for the answers to so many questions that would no doubt reflect my resentment for what had happened 10 years earlier. There was to be no easy way of going about it...another reason I so desperately wanted my sister there. She would know how to do this, I thought to myself.

On the ride from the airport there was little talk and I took advantage of the opportunity that riding in the back seat presented to me to make observations of my step dad and the kind of rapport he and my Mother shared. His occupation as a pipe fitter for Texon lent to his already larger than average physique, his height, at over six feet tall, and his chiseled facial features that made him look more like the Zig Zag man. He was a bit intimidating in appearance, but I quickly reminded myself that he was on my side and that made me relax and feel a whole lot better, and whatever comfort that didn't provide, my little brother made up for. I remember thinking to myself, "it's a good thing Dan isn't here to tell him what a bastard I am." Well...I couldn't help thinking that because he was looking up at me with a kind of adoring admiration that I didn't feel I deserved, or I wasn't sure I ever would deserve, knowing myself and the kind of brother I had already been to Dan. One of the things that Dorothy had explained to me was that it had been easier to locate my Mother because my Grandmother Christine just happened to still be living I the same house she had lived in from the time I was five. What I didn't know was that Granny was staying with Aunt Irene and that my Mother was now renting the very same house, in the very same neighborhood and with most of the very same neighbors, all of which had known me as little Mark. Of course now all of those people who use to play with little Mark were all grown up and seeing little Mark for the first time since my disappearance ten years ago, all the way down to the clerk at Harry's Market. Did I remember any of these people? No, but they sure knew me as little Marky who disappeared ten years ago. I'm sure the outstanding question in all of their minds had to have been where's Marie? We did disappear together but no one ever asked me about her.

My first sight of the house was like stepping back in time. In fact, the entire neighborhood was completely unchanged except that things seemed a lot smaller than they were when I was 5. Walking into the house made me want to be 5 years old again. I seemed to remember the layout of the house as well as the neighborhood much better than the faces of those I had left behind. Perhaps it was being so near the ocean that gave the air a scent that triggered all of the emotions and memories that I had experienced as a child, but from the moment I walked into the house I began to experience a slow motion déjà vu. Much like at the airport but not nearly as slow and with an overwhelming familiarity. My hands seemed to swell and everything sounded like I was hearing it through an empty paper towel tube. Maybe it was an automated psychological reaction to my great desire to delay things down to a pace I felt more comfortable with. Because more than anything I wanted to slow this whole thing down and savor it as I took it all in. But it was hard to do without seeming indifferent and detached, because I was.

Everyone just seemed to take my feelings for granted, going out of their way to accommodate me. None of it was any big deal to them, same house, same neighborhood. What I wanted most was to sit down with my Mom and Uncle Bobby and find out what happened and what had been happening for the past ten years, but my Mom seemed to shield herself with my step dad Steve. Worst of all she seemed in no hurry to offer any explanation. I had been waiting 10 years to know, something...anything. It all seemed to hinge on how happy everyone was to have me back. Never mind how it had all happened and no one even asked about Marie. I knew that since Dorothy knew where Marie was, then my Mom had to also know or at the very least they had to have had some discussion concerning her. So why not talk with me about how this was all unfolding for Marie? When it comes right down to it I don't think there is very much my Mother could have done right in my eyes to change how I felt and I'll be the first to say, there is certainly no way to take it all back because like they say, "the damage is done." But you know what...I don't think saying "that" and then letting it go at "that" is enough to make up for 10 years of being pissed off at the world without even the benefit of knowing why. I really didn't know how to approach the issue so for the first week or two I just tried to enjoy being there, back together with my Mom, in that house with my new brother and among all my family members. We went to the drive-in, had some fun picnics, watched Steve play at a couple of baseball games and, as it turns, I discovered that I didn't have to "try" at all. I ended up having fun pretty damned effortlessly. My Mother and I seemed to have been born with the same quick wit and often cracked jokes on cue with one another. Our personalities and senses of humor are quite parallel and we both seem to know how to appreciate it.

On a day just hanging around the house, my Mom turned to me and said, "ya know your Father will be coming to see you next week." "No Way! I don't have any desire to see him", I said. "Really? Mark, he is your father!" "Fuck him", I said. "Oh Mark, he just wants to see you and spend a little time with you while you're here." Now the first thing that caused a red flag in that statement for me was "while you're here" because it was from that moment I knew I wouldn't be staying and living with Mom. You might think that I would have been heartbroken having not even been offered the option to stay, but quite the contrary; a great weight had been lifted from my shoulders because I had no intension of staying. My mother must have sensed it because I don't honestly think it was a matter of her wanting me to go, but you didn't have to be a genius to see that it would never have worked. I mean, here I was at 15 having lived the past 10 years of my life in a household where I came and went from at my convenience, in an environment with no male figure to answer to, a refrigerator that was always stocked and I talked to Dorothy however I wanted and most of the time not very nicely. All my friends were in Idaho, I was the singer in a Rock-N-Roll

Band and was basically very mouthy, cocky and spoiled rotten from years of using my anger as an excuse to think I had some right to do whatever I wanted. There's only one person on earth that would put up with my shit and that's Dorothy. Besides that, I knew in the back of my mind that a confrontation with my Mother was inevitable, I also knew it would be explosive and guess what folks…it was!

26

I agreed to see and spend some time with my Father over the Fourth of July weekend, 1982. I didn't want to and though I would never have admitted it then, I was afraid! Waiting for him to show up that night was hell and when he finally did show there was no mistaking his knock. It was just like the knock I had heard the day Grandpa chased him off with a kitchen knife. I was on the couch listening to a Bad Company album when I heard the knock and looked in the direction of the front door to see only his feet and legs, only up to the kneecap, through the glass. My Mom didn't tell me much about what to expect, just that he wasn't really all there. I wouldn't answer the door so my Mother opened it and when she did, oh boy, I knew she wasn't lying about him not really being all there. My best recollection of the sight? Chris Farley in a really large, loud tourist shirt or maybe John Candy in Planes, Trains, and Automobiles...either description works. I mean this guy's huge and he's wearing at least a half a bottle of cologne, probably to avoid that "fat guy after a flight of stairs odor." In any event, here's Mom, "Hi Randy, come on in...good to see ya!" How ya been? Nice cologne (wink, wink) Hey, new shirt? (double wink, wink)." I'm thinkin', "come on Mom, let's get this over with." I reluctantly stand and Mom motions that I should hug the guy...so I do. This guy's cologne is strong. It ain't cheap, but it's too strong. He says he's got a room down at the Don Motel. It's only a couple of blocks away. It's the 4th of July and he really hasn't given much thought to how we're going to spend this "time" together...so Mom obliges with a suggestion, "well Rosie and Joe (the neighbor) are taking Chris (my brother) along with their boy down to the Pike in Long Beach for a birthday party, and then their gonna watch the fireworks display over the ocean." That'll work!

I can't remember how we got there, cab or bus, he didn't have a car so it had to have been one of the two. Once there though, man, it was packed with people and families having picnics and parties and barbecues...you name it. It was so packed, in fact, that it took a little while to find Joe and Rosie. It was hard to distinguish one party from the next, but we finally did find them. Most of the kids, including my brother, were a lot younger than me. Rosie and Joe really did a great job at this party; they could tell I was a little uncomfortable so they offered me a couple of wine coolers to take the edge off. Yee Haw...I started drinkin' them babies like Kool Aid, but I was afraid to get too carried away, mostly because I was 15. I didn't know how far to go with it, but good ole Joe kept givin' me the green light... so...hell, me and ole Joe were gettin' drunk while Dad was tearin' up the pork-n-beans. It was a hoot watchin' all them little kids blindfolded and trying to hit that piñata. They were havin' a hell of a time trying to hit the mark. I think Rosie got a little nervous when Joe and I started poppin' off with, "come on, let me take a swing." She got between the piñata and us in a hurry. My Dad really didn't seem to mind about the drinkin' and he cared less about my

154

smokin'. By the time the kids busted open the piñata and we all got to watch the little ones rush in to collect the falling candy, it was getting dark. Ya know, I really must say there is something very special about watching little ones rush in all happy, excited and wide-eyed at the candy falling from a piñata. I felt myself grow up a little, just watching. As it continued to get dark, we all set out to find the best place to watch the fireworks. As a result, my Father and I sort of lost track of Joe and Rosie, but not Christopher. He stayed with my Dad and I, until the last minute before the fireworks started, but he had to regroup with Joe and Rosie. I don't know how he ever found them, but he did. This was a fantastic firework display! It was long and truly beautiful. All in all, I had a great time. We caught a cab back to the Don Hotel and trudged up to his room.

Suddenly, I found myself alone in a motel room with a man I had once been afraid to death of, but by this time, he was too fat to be afraid of. I really didn't know what to say. He turned the TV on and we sat and watched in an uncomfortable silence for what seemed like an eternity, until I came up with an idea. I looked over at him and said, "lets get drunk"…and much to my surprise he simply answered with a smile and asked, "what's your favorite kind of beer?" I gave it a moment of thought and barked out, "Heineken, but we don't have to get that." "No, No, No…we can get that…two cases sound good", he asked? In the next scene we were rollin' two cases of Heineken back to the motel in a shopping cart. Once we got back up to the room, I cleared the little table, grabbed the little tumbler glass and proceeded with a crash course called "Quarters 101." I said, "Okay, all ya gotta do is bounce this here quarter off the table and into the glass. If you make it, I have to drink and you go again until you miss, then it's my turn." He took a turn at it and missed. Oops...'cause I didn't miss until he had the first six-pack down. Poor guy, he was gettin' hammered, but don't worry, so was I. Remember, I had a head start!

We drank until the room was littered with beer cans. Yea, "cans", that's all the store had. Before too long ole Randy C was rollin' around on the bed like a big ole beached walrus, moaning with hunger pains, "ooooh Rime Rungry ooooh". What the hell, I was up for a walk so I said, "hey there's a Taco Bell down on Avalon, just a couple blocks from here." Boy he jumped up like Scooby Doo does for a Scooby snack...Raco Rell? Off we went...stumbling down the sidewalk. I'd get a little ahead of him and say, "come on, just a couple more blocks", but I knew damned well it was a lot further. Mean? Uh, uh...here was a chance I didn't think I would ever have, to impose a little suffering on a man I had watched physically abuse my Mom; not to mention his girlfriend in my presence, plus inflict a lot of mental pain on all of us. I saw an opportunity to make his fat ass walk a little further, which I might add, did appear to cause him great discomfort, so I took advantage of it. Nothing to the kind of discomfort he had imposed on so many people over the years, but, with all of that animosity aside, there is

156

one thing I will always be forever grateful to Randy C for, and that is my gift for music. I got it from him.

My Dad wasn't always the man he is today. Not only did he also sing in Rock-n-Roll bands, but my mother, Becky, told me that he was once a very high spirited and entertaining fellow to be around. What happened? Well, I'll give you my theory, but do me a favor...try to keep in mind that that's all it is, a theory. I wasn't there to see things unfold for Randy C, but I think the guy quite simply made some really bad choices and did some of the kinds of things that people rarely, if ever, forgive themselves for and I don't think he ever did, but check this out...if God can forgive him (and I know he can), then so do I. I'll never feel sorry for him and even though I'm not very religious, I'm not above or below forgiveness. Well, that wasn't easy, but it sure felt good! How about that?

Now, where the hell was I (no pun intended). We finally made it to Taco Bell. I thought he was gonna die, but it's amazing what 3 Burrito Supremes can do for a fat guy. We really didn't talk much about anything; there really wasn't much to talk about. Once back at the Don he passed out hard core, so there I was with about a case of beer to drink. I did the best I could by playing quarters with myself until I passed out on the floor. I still woke up before him, but it was almost checkout time, so I woke him up reluctantly. It was sort of like pokin' at a body with a stick, except I used a hanger...Randy...Randy...hey, it's almost check out time and Mom's gonna be worried. He sat up and rubbed his eyes. He asked if I wanted a cab and I said no, I could walk; it's only a couple blocks. He said, "okay" and then hugged me. He was doing his best to keep it together but I could feel his heartbeat quicken and his big body start to shake during the hug. Strangely, it affects me more now as I write about it than it did at that moment, but let's stick to that moment. At that very moment, I really didn't feel anything except an anxiousness to get back to my Mom's. As we broke from the hug, I could see he was crying and all I could do was look away. My feelings were so mixed and confused, I didn't know what to say or do or feel. You see, I didn't know this man at all and yet I had spent an entire evening with him not talking about anything in particular, drinking and just hanging out and now here he was, standing in front of me, crying, and having a hard time saying good-bye. What was I suppose to feel? He took off his watch and gave it to me. This was an expensive watch. I didn't know what to say except, "no" but that didn't work...as he insisted, as if to say, it was the last time he would ever see me and wanted me to have something to remember him by. I still said, "no", but the maid was at the door now..."check out time, me clean woom now"...knock, knock, knock!! It was time, so I gave him one last handshake and a brief hug and then opened the door to the wide-eyed maid who saw the mess and said, "you go now, you weave big mess, you drink too many beer...you go now, so can clean!" "Bye Dad", I said as I skipped past the maid and smiled. As I walked down the hall to the elevator,

I could still hear the maid, "that your son, him too young drink beer! What matter you? You go now!" "Ding!" The elevator opened and I stepped on, alone.

27

It's strange how an old elevator enhances anxieties and emotion, especially when going down. All kinds of thoughts rushed through my mind on that walk home, but most of it was confusion. What just happened? Well…here's what I think happened, ready? First…you've got the man whom hasn't seen his son for 10 years, wanting to reunite, and second you've got the son whose thoughts on the idea are apparently not important enough for him to be asked…and when his thoughts are expressed they are ignored. As a result the son winds up in a screwy situation that, if you ask me, and that's "if"…does a lot more harm than good and more so for Dad. Sure Dad gets to see son, but ya know what, I could have gone a lifetime without having that scenario sprung on me, ya know? (Sometimes it's not about me.)

When I got to Mom's there were questions, like: "how come he made me walk? how did it go? what did we talk about?" I didn't answer any of them, not even the first of which I could have. I was so weirded out about the whole experience, I didn't know how to feel…let alone how to answer, and since I didn't answer, guess what? Mom thought I was being a little jerk, which might have been an easy assumption when it's all about Mom, but it wasn't all about Mom, and I wasn't being a little jerk, just for the sake of dis'en Mom. I was being a little jerk because I felt bombarded with questions I was still trying to figure out answers for. Answers for questions I never wanted to have to answer in the first place. I felt like a guinea pig. First, thrust into a scenario by her and then poked and prodded with questions about the experience by her. How dare I not answer her questions. Immediately she got an attitude. I didn't blow up at first...no...I let it stew for a couple of days, but a couple of days was it! For those couple of days there was tension between my Mother and I. Thank God Uncle Bobby was hangin' around. He didn't ask any questions and for the next couple of days we did things like hitchhike to the beach, play Frisbee in the underground pedestrian X-ing and got drunk down the street with some black kids from the neighborhood.

Well, I got drunk...Bobby doesn't drink. Bobby and his wife, Aunt Linda, had an apartment not far from my Mom's house. Bobby had gone inside for a few minutes and I decided to wait outside and while I did three black kids approached me. "Well, well, well, look like we got us a little white boy done found hisself ina rong nebahood." "Hey man, I'm just waitin' on my Uncle Bobby", I said. "Bobby? You mean downstairs Bobby, you his nephew? Yea...daaamn... you all right then. Say we bout ta hit the liquor store, ya'll want to throw in wit us on some Colt." I said sure, I could use a beer so I gave em my last 5 bucks. By the time they made it back and handed me my quart of Colt 45, without the change, Bobby still hadn't made it out, but I didn't care I was kickin'it, I was cool. We were all four drinkin' in the concrete barbecue area, complete with broken down cinder block wall where a car had crashed through it at one time, when a little red Toyota with three white kids rolled up real slow. The driver rolled his window down and asked if there was any weed around. The oldest black kid motioned him to pull up and park. So he did. The kid was havin a hard time letting his money go with the neighborhood kid so all of the sudden I was asked over to the car. The next thing I heard was, "Come on now white boy, I'll even leave you with one of your kind to wait in the car with you while I run wit yo money. I ain't goin' no where...Mark, he cool, he ain't gonna let notin happin to yo cash...Mark wait here with these white boys while I go get em some bud." With that, the kid handed him the money and I jumped in the back seat to wait. I lit up a cigarette and asked where they were from. One of them said in a nervous voice, "not from around here, that's for sure." These kids were scared. I could feel it. My thoughts were confirmed when the driver asked me how to get to the nearest freeway on ramp so they could get out of this area as soon as possible. I just kinda chuckled when I told him how to get there. I guess because of my having family and having lived there myself, it really never occurred to me that I might be in a dangerous neighborhood, so I found it amusing. I don't know why but I tried to put their minds at ease, probably because it made me feel like a tough guy to publicize that I wasn't afraid and they were. It certainly wasn't because I was sure the black kid was coming back with their weed, because I wasn't sure at all, but he did, and they were outta there. About the time they were pulling away, Bobby walked up and, let me tell ya, he did not take too kindly to the sight of me hangin' with these black kids. Not that Uncle Bobby is racist but he knew these kids and he was worried about them rippin' me off or getting me into some kind of bullshit hustle, you know, the kind that had just pulled away in that little red Toyota. Of course, I had already been ripped off for my change from the Colt 45's. When Uncle Bobby learned that I had givin' them my money for the beer, he did the math quickly and was all up in the oldest kids face. "Where's my nephew's change?" I said, "hey hey hey, it's cool Bobby...we all just wanted a beer so I bought ...it's cool, take it easy, they haven't ripped me off." "Yea, so what you gonna do anyway", the kid said...I answered his question for him when I said, "hey man, do yourself a favor...don't push your luck, 'cause if I say you ripped me off, Bobby will fuck all 3 of you up...no problem!" Well, they must have taken my word for it because all he did was light up a joint and pass it to me. As you can imagine the whole idea of kickin' it and drinking beer with these guys was, oh shall I say, soured. So, I took a couple more hits off the joint and Bobby and I headed back up to Mom's house. We hung out there for the rest of the night.

The next day there was still an air of tension going on between my Mother and I, which in turn really made it very difficult to be a big brother to my new brother Chris...and let me tell you he did everything in an effort to get my attention. Unfortunately, his efforts were in vain. I was so preoccupied with the simmering unresolved issues between our Mother and I that I never gave him the time of day...also something our Mom was perturbed about. What the hell was I supposed to do? What she did? Act like every thing was all right now, fall into step without missing a beat and then play the part of Greg Brady? As far as I was concerned, we still had some unfinished business. I don't know what started it that day but somehow I ended up calling her a "fuckin bitch" oops! something I had been calling Dorothy to her face for years...so you can imagine my astonishment when I got slapped. Well, if you can imagine that, then imagine her astonishment when I went to slap her back. Even though she blocked me, it was on...we were throwing blows. I heard her call for Bobby and that's when I ran. I ran as fast as I could, down the street, through an alley and up a tree. I lost him but I could see him walking around down there calling my name, "Mark, where'd ya go? Mark, I just want to talk to you...come on Mark!" I stayed up there in that tree crying until it got dark, not knowing what to do. I wanted to scream up at the sky again, but I couldn't...somebody might have seen me up there. Finally, I just climbed down and wiped my face off and put on my best tough guy act before walking back to the house. I was greeted by a teary eyed Mother, who had been worried sick and that made me feel pretty good. No, not that I had caused her to worry, but that I was welcomed back with no hard feelings. Hey, ya never know.

28

A couple of days later I was on my way to LAX for my plane ride back to Boise, ID. I assured my Mom and brother I would be back. They didn't want to see me go, but at the same time I don't think my Mom knew and may have even been a bit leery about knowing how to deal with the big monster inside of little Mark. The entire experience grew me up in ways I wasn't sure of or even aware of and as a whole left me with a little less of the brand of bitterness I was accustomed to, but at the same time introduced me to a new hardened sense of confused bitterness. This new maturity, in my best description, was a mirror that reflected me to myself with such clarity that I had no choice but to acknowledge the fact that I had been extremely lucky to be adopted by Dorothy. Not to suggest that I would have been unlucky to be raised by my natural mother, but by the time we were reunited I was already stuck in my ways. The catch to this new enlightenment and maturity meant that my conscience was going to be holding me more accountable for what I thought was "okay" to be bitter about. In short, it meant I wouldn't be able to stomach any continuation of being the punk I had been, for the same flimsy justifications knowing how spoiled I had been. My feelings at the time were, "dammit!" this means I'll have to come up with better justifications for being volatile and angry all of the time. The feeling was only a panicky reaction to being unfamiliar with the kinds of benefits that accompany the kind of insight- full maturity I had begun to experience.

The first benefit came in a form that was more precious than gold. Priceless in fact! As I mentioned in earlier chapters, I had through the years been somewhat of a bully to my brother Dan. Upon my return from Los Angeles, I was somewhat surprised when I noticed a difference in the brother who had always been somewhat of a loner. Not only had he physically matured, but also he had socially matured from "Drooler Boy" to a guy with friends and his own sense of coolness. One night we had an argument about something or other and to my amazement Dan popped off with the comment, "hey fucker, I'll take you out in front and beat your head up against the house". I was impressed and intrigued with his new set of balls so I obliged him and said, "after you". I followed him out front and we squared off, I put my dukes up and I said, "start beatin motherfucker!" The problem here was that I had also changed. Where once I had been the brother who would have initiated the physical attack, I now stood there and left it up to him. He was caught completely off guard by this and said, "fuck dude, I can't just hit ya". That's when I walked up to him and looked him straight in the eyes and said, "now you know what an asshole I feel like for being a jerk to you all these years." As I walked away I began to realize the benefit of the insightful maturity I had so recently acquired, and since that day there hasn't been a harsh word between us.

In that single moment I had felt my life begin to change, but I was far from being anything that even resembled the word "humble". I began to practice with the band again and one night, shortly after arriving home from Toni's, I got a phone call from the last person on Earth I would have expected...Sheila R. I was caught off guard by this considering I hadn't given her my phone number, but not just that, it was that she had said more to me in the first 30 seconds of the call then she had said during the entire night I had last seen her. To tell you the truth I didn't expect to ever see or talk to her again after the weird night with Willie W. Her voice was charged with energy. It seems she had been trying to reach me all week and I explained that I had been in Los Angeles. She then went on to tell me that Willie had been arrested and was in jail in Mountain Home and that it was our responsibility to try and bust him out of jail. I said, "uh, Sheila, you're crazy", no that's not true... what I really said was "Jean you're crazy", because for some reason, and to this day I don't know why, Jean was the name she went by. I should have mentioned much earlier in the book that it wasn't until much later that I would use her given name Sheila. Anyway, I said, "Jean you're crazy". She said, "I know but there's got to be something we can do, I feel bad". She sounded way too sarcastic and flirtatious to feel bad for poor Willie W and I decided to play along just for the sake of listening to her speak. Remember, this phone call was the first taste of what flavor her personality was beyond the rolling of her eyes at Wizards Arcade. My way of playing along was pretty direct. I said, "no you don't", she said, "yes I do", "no ya don't", "yes I do", "no ya don't"... until we both bustin' up laughing and she finally admitted, "okay, you're right, I don't". By that time there was chemistry in our conversation and at about that same time I noticed a Select-A-Seat envelope on the kitchen counter. It hit me that Dorothy had asked me if I was interested in going to the upcoming Heart/Loverboy concert at the then new Boise State Pavilion. She had left two tickets for me in the envelope. So I says, "hot damn", looky here, July 17th at the Boise State Pavilion, Heart with special guest Loverboy," in my best Gary Owens radio announcer voice and she was laughing at the way I had asked her to go. She said she would be happy to come along and we concluded the conversation with a lingering chemistry that made it hard to say goodbye. Needless to say Dorothy was my unwitting hero that week.

On July 17th, 1983, I found myself walking in circles through the corridors of the pentagon shaped Boise State Pavilion with Sheila (Jean) R. I don't think we watched any of the concert, but instead spent the time talking and joking and laughing and exploring each other's personalities and from that night forward we were inseparable. The chemistry was killing me and I wanted to kiss her so bad but a little voice in the back of my head kept saying, this isn't the kind of girl that Willie W or anybody for that matter is going to lose lying down. I had to remind myself of the way he had treated her and that if he cared at all he wouldn't be in jail... besides, she called me!

So after all of this reasoning with myself, I finally asked her what was going on with their relationship. She said they were done, and with that I could feel my palms start to sweat and my heart skipped several times. The adrenaline and anticipation that led up to our first kiss was something I'll never forget and the kiss itself was even better. "So, would it be all right to kiss ya, I asked sheepishly?" "Yea, you can kiss me." So we kissed, and kissed, and kissed...in fact we were still kissing as we both simultaneously sat down on the floor and kissed some more. At a glance we were an unlikely couple. Sheila was always impeccably dressed and probably taller than me with heels. I rarely wore anything fancier than white Nikes, 501's and some concert T-shirt, likely from either Journey or Def Leopard's last tour. I'm gonna take a gamble here and say that she was attracted to my personality and my charisma...if I'm wrong, sue me! Whatever it was, it was enough to make her want to be with me all the time and I felt the same for her. So if she wasn't staying at my house then I was staying at hers.

My house was easy because I usually had the run of it, but Sheila's house was another story completely. You see Sheila has a Dad...not just any Dad but an extremely eccentric and sometimes intimidating Dad. Now don't get me wrong, Sheila's Dad is cool, it's just that he doesn't always like ya to know it, especially at first. Sheila's Mom was an absolute sweetheart. We wanted to be together all the time but we were afraid to approach Sheila's Dad about me staying there, so we would wait for the most opportune time to sneak me into her house and then I would stay in her room, sometimes for days without coming out. Sometimes during the day, if her Dad were home, I would sneak out her window and then come around to the front door and knock as if I was just dropping by. Sheila's Mom knew what we were doing and we thought we were pretty slick getting over on Dad until one day, when I was just "dropping by", ole Dad answered the door and said, "come on in". I sat down next to him on the couch, he offered me a beer and as he handed me one…in a real casual voice he says, "yea…you gotta watch that toilet seat boy". Trouble was I hadn't been to the can. "Oops, dammit"…I was busted, but he was cool about it and as we talked he seemed to be taking an interest in getting to know me and I was really surprised at how well we actually did get along. I think he hadn't seen his daughter take such risks just to be with someone before and probably wanted to gage my worthiness for himself. His way of doing it was by getting drunk with me and befriending me in a way that would get me to open up about myself to him…like any father would. He wanted to know a little about my background, my belief structure, my ethics and my integrities. These were things I didn't mind sharing with him because it has always been important to me that people know at least enough about me to know that I'm not a predator and that I don't have malicious intent. I'm not out to get anyone, however, when it came to the big question, "what do I want to do with your life", he nailed me, because not only did I not have an answer for that, but I had always resented the concept that a person should have to know what they want to do... particularly at 16. Obviously things were pretty serious between his daughter and I since she was sneaking me in and hiding me out like she had been. My answer was the wrong answer and it came across with the wrong disposition. At that age I was still very interested in hearing a good justification for why somebody has to know what they want to do in life, so I figured hell, we're friends now...what better person to ask. Throw in a couple of beers and a personality that doesn't allow me to close my mouth when I should, and you've got yourself a real "Daddy Pleaser". My attitude about the whole thing sort of set me up as a condescending opponent, more than anything else, and I think my use of the word "justification" in the same context as the question says it all about where my head was at. However, all was not lost thanks to the fact that Sheila had the good sense to be listening and to know where and when it was time to pull me into her room and not let me back out until we were leaving, therefore preventing the whole train wreck. After that day I was welcome to stay from time to time, but Dad's knowing gave me sort of an eerie feeling. I'm quite sure this was caused by the fact that whenever I was there I never wanted to come out of her room. Her father's knowledge of my presence made me uncomfortable. Maybe it's because he made me feel like I needed to be visiting with him more of the time than I wanted to. It would have been more appropriate for obvious reasons but I didn't want to, I was there to be with Sheila, not hang with Pop. Sheila seemed to feel it too and, as a result, she began staying at my house more of the time and to me this was wonderful because it meant that I had her all to myself in my kingdom. The only drawback was that by this time Rick was back from the Army and was sharing my room with me.

This was a big room and it wasn't as bad as it sounds. From what I could tell the only thing Rick learned in the army was how to drink and they did a much better job at teaching him how to inhale cigarettes...to the tune of about 2 ½ packs a day...which was cool with me because it meant he always had cigarettes and booze so we got along just fine. The fact that I seemed to be one of the few who could keep up with his drinking made our relationship all the more copasetic. Most of the time Sheila and I had the room to ourselves and whenever Rick was there, he, as usual, passed out. As time went on, Sheila began to become more and more acquainted with the various circles of friends already in my life, since we never went anywhere without one another. She seemed to have few of her own friends, but the operative word here is "seemed".

Her name was no less notorious than mine, but I think she just opted to spend her time with me and I had enough friends for both of us. She would come to band practice with me and go with me to the parties where the band would play. She got to know all of my friends in Nampa, including Danny D and his girlfriend at the time, Michelle. Now for some reason I didn't like the idea of Sheila going out with Michelle by herself. The fact is I didn't like her going "out" anywhere without me, but on one particular night, I was dead set against it. It was the first time she had ever shown an independent desire to go have fun without me so I was shocked, appalled, hurt but worst of all I was drunk...very drunk! We were both quite hammered, which was one of the reasons I didn't want her to go with Michelle. It just seemed so out of character for her to want to leave anyway. Well, the argument started across the street from Spunkies in the parking lot in front of 7-11. I don't know what she said, probably, "I'm going", but it sent me running toward her. I grabbed her arms and began shaking her...as I said, we were both very intoxicated and at some point she had lost her balance and fell backwards with me falling directly on top of her. Before I could get up on my own I was being jerked up by a police officer, handcuffed, placed under arrest for domestic battery and stuffed into a police car. Boy, you should have seen Sheila go off on this cop. "Let him go you fucking pig, it was an accident...he didn't do anything." She was kicking and swinging on the cop and when he finally restrained her he threatened to arrest her for battery on an officer if she didn't calm down. Michelle and Danny got her to calm down enough to follow us down to the police station and call Dorothy to see what she could do about getting me out. It took some convincing by Sheila that it really was an accident, because I can imagine what it must have looked like to the officer, but they were finally

173

convinced and dropped all charges letting me go that night. Thank you Sheila. After that incident we took a break from each other and it was during that break, while partying with my Nampa circle of friends, that I flushed it all down the toilet...I was unfaithful. It was the dumbest thing I could have done, well—almost the dumbest.

I think my getting arrested for DUI the following week was really what sealed it. I went to jail and stayed there because, by getting arrested, I had also violated my probation, so there was no bail. Glenn E was no longer my probation officer, having transferred my case to Nampa. My new PO was a woman I had never met and it took about 6 weeks before I even knew her name. During this time Sheila wrote to me fanatically. Sometimes I would receive 4 or 5 letters on a single day, all saturated with Jovan Musk for Women. I thought I was going to loose my mind and I wanted to die. I was ridden with guilt about what I had done, but I needed her correspondence so desperately that I didn't dare jeopardize it with a mere written confession. I also knew she was hanging around with many of the people whom knew of my indiscretion. Combined with not knowing what was going to happen in court, I was an emotional mess. In late October of 1983, the court decided my fate and by Nov. 8th back to St. Anthony I went.

29

I was housed in Bitterroot this time, the cottage for returnees and the oldest kids, and I went straight into solitary confinement. The extent of my dialogue was, "fuck you". I was just plain hateful. I had been in solitary confinement about 2 months when one day I heard a commotion at my cell door, keys jingling and a woman's voice saying "what the hell's the matter with you people?" I didn't know what the hell was going on but before I knew it I was looking up at a woman...a very big woman. She was looking down at me with my file in her hand. She said, "guess what Mr. Snowball, you're getting out of this cell today and being put in the mainstream population." I said, "Fuck you!! I ain't goin' nowhere." She took one step forward and backed me into the corner of my bunk. She lowered her head and looked me straight in the eyes and said, "Randy, that's not going to work anymore. I'm takin' you out of here and whether you like it or not you're coming into my office for one hour every day...and we're going to discuss Randy Snowball." I yelled at her, "fuck you!" She looked back at the male guard and motioned that she should be left alone with me. The guard shrugged and walked away. She took yet another step forward into my space and by now I was really cornered in a ball on my bunk. There was no getting away from this big woman and she continued to inch closer and closer - very slowly - until finally she extended both of her arms and said, "honey, it's alright I want to help you." I couldn't help myself; I lost control and burst into tears. She took one final step forward, pulled me into her arms and as she held me I wept while she repeated, "it's alright Randy, I'm gonna help you get through all of this, but you've got to come out of here." The more she spoke the harder I wept but she never let go and she allowed me all the time I needed to bawl my eyes out... When I could finally regain my composure, we walked out of that cell together with the promise I would see her at 4:00 o'clock the next day in her office. The woman's name is Barbara F and by 4:00 o'clock PM the next day my defiant disposition had returned full force and I had to be escorted into her office kicking and screaming every vulgar cuss word you could imagine. Once inside the tiny office, we were left to ourselves and the first thing Barbara did was lock the door behind me trapping me inside and then placing the key in her bra. When I realized what she had done I flew into a rage, kicking chairs and throwing books in all directions. Her reaction was to casually sit down in her chair, kick her legs up onto her desk, light up a cigarette and turn the pages of my file as if she were reviewing it, always calm and completely unaffected by whatever I did. In fact, she seemed to have anticipated my behavior. There was no amount of book throwing, yelling or name calling that could shake or surprise Barbara. She seemed to be even more confident than I was, knowing me well enough to be certain I wouldn't cross the line into physically attacking her. After about 5 or so minutes of this, I would become exhausted. I would turn over a chair and sit in it winded from the amount of energy I had exerted. She blew out a puff of smoke and said, "tired ain't cha?" I wouldn't say anything but just give her my best tough guy stare. She countered with, "ya know Randy, it takes an incredible amount of energy to be angry all the time and I'll bet you're exhausted and I don't mean from just that little tantrum, I mean I'll bet when you lay down at night you go right to sleep and you wake up tired." She was right on the money but I wasn't about to admit to it and I responded with, "fuck you." She blew out another puff of smoke, crushed out her cigarette and without the slightest indication that what I had said had affected her in anyway, without looking up she opened a file on her desk, began to look at it and said, "are you done?" All I could think about was "*what*" in the world I was gonna have to do or say to get under this woman's thick skin. I blurted out another "fuck you" but this time it was more out of nervousness than contempt. Then she said something that really threw me. She said, "are you sure you're Randy Snowball? Randolph Mark Casey Snowball? I want to be sure about his because according to this file the guy I'm supposed to be talking to is a lot smarter than to act like whoever "you" are. Oh yea, it says here the guy I'm looking for has a higher than average IQ, is a self taught pianist, can sing beautifully and is even somewhat of a comedian when he wants to be, but that doesn't at all match up with the asshole sitting across from me." "I don't give a fuck what you or anyone else thinks about me", I snapped. Boy she set me up for that one with the "asshole" remark. She knew well in advance

177

how I would react and had her own response ready. She looked at me and in a sweet calm voice said, "honey that's a lot of garbage and you may have convinced yourself into believing it but I happen to know that we all care very much about what other people think of us and that includes you. Nobody wants to be disliked or shunned by his or her peers." I said, "I do". She lit up another cigarette and said, "sweetheart, you're a lot smarter than that." She blew out a cloud of smoke, leaned back in her chair and said, "honey I've got nothing but time so you've got to make a decision. If you want to get out of this institution you're going to have to let me in, open up and the sooner you begin to do that the sooner you're going to begin to feel better about yourself and the way you feel inside about not trusting people. I know you're tired, I can see it in your eyes and I also know you're afraid." Everything she was saying to me was a direct hit and with every bulls-eye my wall began to weaken and crumble. She went on to continually compliment my intelligence and for this I had no defense...you can't say "fuck-you" to someone who keeps telling you how smart you are. Gradually I started to break down and cry and as I did so she began to cry with me. She came over and hugged me and as she held me close to her big body she assured me that nobody around here is going to make fun of you for crying, and then she pulled away, hands still on my shoulders and said, "Randy, you're talented, you're smart and if I were 20 years younger I'd be your girlfriend because you're also a very handsome young man."

I couldn't help laughing and blushing, the remark helped me pull myself together and we both silently returned to our seats. There was a brief pause, a simultaneous blushing glance exchanged and then we both just chuckled as she handed me a Kleenex from her desk. We both dried our faces and she concluded with, "tomorrow...4:00 o'clock now get outta here kiddo." I had never met anyone like Barbara F. She really seemed to know where I was coming from, what I felt and she wasted no time crashing through my barriers. The more she reminded me of how smart I was, the easier the realizations and acceptances became. There's quite a difference between when you're asked how you feel and when you're told, wouldn't you agree? She was a gracious, caring therapist. By gracious I mean that when it came to letting me speak about the way things were and had been affecting me, she always gave me the floor and enough time to express it in the manner that was most comfortable to me. I was never rushed and always felt that my thoughts and expressions were valuable to her...and when I feel like that, I become eager to share. Not only did I become eager to hear her comments and advice, but as a result of the trust in our relationship, it started to become much easier for me to sit and listen to the things I didn't like to hear. What I began to figure out was that most of the valuable lessons in life come from circumstances and people we don't like...but the pain is in the knowing. There are times I have wished I weren't smart enough to have to know or that I could just go through life being ignorant, never quite getting it. If given a choice between a lifetime of struggling through my own ignorance or struggling through the pain of knowing, I'm afraid I would have to opt for the latter because I can't imagine cheating myself out of how it feels to evolve in my own introspection. As long as the mind stays "open", this fascinating meta-physical experience of self-evolution never ends.

My second stay at St. Anthony was vastly different from the first, meeting Barbara saved my life! Our daily discussions about Randy Snowball made it possible for me to step outside of myself and see myself in a way that proved invaluable in terms of my capacity to realize how truly exhausted I had become with my own anger. Unbeknownst to me I had reached a dead end with it and as a result of not knowing where to go or what to do with it all, I was only getting madder and more hostile. I hated myself for putting myself there…I knew I was smart enough to know better but I didn't know what to do until Barbara came along. I felt as though I had no control of the anger, but the hour a day with Barbara F opened up a side of myself I had never known existed. She was a light at the end of the tunnel that provided just the right brand of disarming self-gratification at just the right time of my life.

Now lets face it…the entire reason I went straight into solitary confinement was because I was pissed off at the world and myself for having put myself in a situation that took me away from Sheila. I was in love with her, or at least I thought I was...but if that's love then it was the worst kind of love, a "co-dependant/parasitic" love. It's the kind of love that brings you to your knees when you're not with them, or makes your stomach churn to think of them because the longing is so strong. In fact, I was so incredibly pained by this "love" that I never discussed it with Barbara. This was one subject I kept to myself. Barbara seemed to have no knowledge of the issue so I quite simply kept it to myself. There were plenty of other issues that attributed to my attitude and since we made so much progress in those areas, it was easy to hide. I had every intention in being with Sheila when I got released, so the last thing I wanted to hear was that it might not happen that way...and then there was my indiscretion. I prayed everyday she wouldn't find out while I was locked up, but I knew deep down that eventually she would. The stress from that alone was making me age. It wasn't until about 4 months into my stay that I received her letter telling me she had found out, asking me why and then basically dumping me. It was devastating to have to deal with this through the mail; however, by the time it finally happened, I was much more at peace with myself. I won't go as far as to say it was easy, but easier. I felt horrible for abusing her trust all the way up to when she found out. She would send me 4 and 5 letters at a time telling me how much she loved me and how she was waiting. I enjoyed reading them so much; those letters meant the entire world to me, so I just didn't have the balls to give them up by telling her myself. I just couldn't do it! Because of it, I would learn a lesson I would not soon forget. It could not have been easy for her, but I'm not at liberty to discuss her emotional experience during this period of her life...only mine.

It still took me about 8 months to make it through the program at St. Anthony and upon my release I went straight to Sheila, but to no avail. Yes, we spent some time together, but I'll venture to say that it was because she couldn't shake me. I wanted desperately to change the past and make up for my indiscretion, but the damage was done. She would never trust me again and because of the pain I had caused her...in short, it was over. When Sheila left town for the summer to stay with family in Texas, to say I was destroyed was an understatement. Not only was I emotionally destroyed, but a lot of my personal belongings were destroyed in fits of rage. I needed an escape and that's exactly what I did.

After having it out with Dorothy...several times...I finally packed a bag and decided it was time to hit the road. I didn't have any money so before I left I searched Dorothy's room for anything I thought I might be able to sell for food money and I found it in the top right drawer of her dresser, a brand spankin' new .38 caliber revolver. There were no bullets to be found and thank God for that. I tucked the pistol away in my bag and had good ole Rick drop me off on the freeway on-ramp headed west. My destination...Los Angeles.

I didn't have a map and I didn't have a compass, all I knew was that the sun set in the West so that's the direction I headed in. This was an interesting journey and I made it in 4 days. The first ride I got was from an accountant, a pretty laid-back dude. Yea, pretty laid back until at some point during our casual conversation I decided to pull out the pistol and ask "wanna buy a gun, I need some travelin' cash, whatta ya say?" I thought the guy was going to have a heart attack. I guess since I didn't have any bullets, I didn't think anything of it, but of course he didn't know that. As I pulled it from my bag his eyes became filled with fear. He said, "Hey Hey Hey"...I couldn't help but chuckle as I quickly interjected with, "No, No, No... I'm not gonna shoot you man, it's not even loaded; look, see", I clicked open the chamber to prove it was empty and he exhaled hard. There was a brief uncomfortable silence as he drove on. I still couldn't help being amused and I chuckled to myself once again as I put it back in my bag. I looked over and said, "Not interested huh?"-------- "No, gonna have to pass on that one! Listen, I'm gonna go ahead and drop you here in Vale because from there I'm going the other way." I'm thinking "surrrre", but that was okay. He dropped me in Vale, Oregon. I think I was on the highway for only about 10 minutes with my thumb out when an old beat up Ford Econoline van pulled over and stopped. I ran up, opened the door and got in. I turned to face the guy and found myself face to face with an old maniacal looking biker with two wondering eyes and a 3-legged Doberman Pincher in the back. He had long scraggly hair and a long goatee. I stuck my hand out and introduced myself. He didn't respond, just shifted gears and looked over at me with those crazy wondering eyes and said, "I'm gonna stop up here and grab a bite, alright?" We pulled into a little diner and sat down in a booth across from each other. The waitress brought us both menus. She handed him one and went to hand me one, but I motioned that I was fine. He looked up from his menu with those crazy eyes and said, "You ain't got no money do ya?" I lied... "Yea I got money, I'm just not hungry." "Bullshit! now go ahead and get something I'm buyin' ---------- this time." This guy was freakin' me out, and I thought I was going to pee my pants as I took the menu with my shaky hand and nervously ordered a burger and fries. I'll bet the waitress was laughing inside. When she walked away he looked across the table at me and said, "My name is Vernon, where ya headed?" I told him Los Angeles and he said I was in luck and could take me as far as Yreka, California. I asked if that was close or on the way to L.A. He just laughed for the first time and said yes. We finished our food and left the diner. I didn't know it at the time but I was about to ride in this old beat-up van with this freakish looking old biker for the next 500-600 miles. As we drove it wasn't long before I discovered that ole Vernon's appearance was much worse than his bite. In fact, after a bit of discussion ole Vernon told me his full name and it was the combination of his middle and last name that really rang a bell. I asked him if he had a son by those names and if his son had ever gone to reform school at St. Anthony. He said yes. I said "well then.. guess what? --------- I'm friends with your son," and from that point on things were a lot more relaxed. Things were already relaxed, Vernon just liked to play on his looks and freak people out. It took us about 2 days in that old van. I swear I don't think the thing went over 60 mph. Once we got to Yreka, he stopped at some old friends' and while they talked, his friend worked on a Harley. Finally we left there and started driving up into the mountains. We drove for quite awhile until we came upon a pretty good sized "A" framed style log cabin. This place was really out in the boonies and I didn't ask any questions. The place had a big deck and porch and standing on it, waiting to greet us, was an old man that I swear looked like he was right out of one of those old leather bound Civil War Commemorative edition books that you buy on T.V. The old guy had lost one of his legs, from the knee down, so he stood there with a cane and his peg leg that looked more like the leg from a Grand Piano. He looked like a Confederate soldier who'd lost his leg in the war and had to improvise the prosthetic. Nevertheless, these two start hugging like brothers and without words I'm asked to hang around out front on the porch, while they head off into the woods. I didn't have much choice in the matter so I just sat down in a rocking chair and started to daydream but I was quickly startled awake by the sound of gunfire in the distance. I had to assume they were test firing the 38. Then I started thinkin', "shit, these guys might decide to shoot my ass out here and no one would be the wiser." I had to calm down; I didn't want to seem nervous, shit! It might have made them nervous so I talked myself out of that way of thinking. They were out there shooting for a while and when they came back we smoked a joint and Vernon practically had to carry my ass to the van. By the time we left, I was lethargic. We made one more stop at some girl's house, smoked another joint and then he drove me to the highway on-ramp. It was funny the way he kept saying, "Man I don't want to just drop ya, but I don't know what else to do." It was a far cry from the guy who picked me up and I finally just shook his hand and told him to get the hell outta here, and that I would be fine. He really seemed to feel bad about leaving me on that on-ramp....funny!

I got a ride in the first 5 minutes after he pulled away. A Volkswagen bug driven by a guy AWOL from the navy. He was a little late returning from his pass. I couldn't have been luckier because it meant he was going all the way to San Diego and the guy gave me a ride all the way to Los Angeles. I kept him stoned the whole way with the skunk bud (pot) I got for the gun. We got to L.A. and I had to call my mother Becky from a phone booth to ask directions. Getting to L.A. is one thing but knowing which freeway to get on is quite another. By this time she had moved out of Grannies old house, but the new house wasn't far from the old one and I had no problem finding it. In fact, I got dropped off in the driveway.

31

I was welcomed with open arms by my Mom, Chris and Steve. I didn't know how long I would stay or even what I was doing but I needed to clear my head from what was going on in Idaho and thank God they didn't ask a whole lot of questions with regard to my plans, because at that point I would not have had any answers. It was during this visit that I learned that my Mother had been granted custody of my sister Marie as a result of the annulment of the adoption from Vivian T. I knew in my heart that there was uneasiness in Marie whenever I went to stay with her on visits to Vivian's house in Acton. What I would learn years later was that Vivian had been beating my sister during those younger years and that the annulment was a direct result of the fact that Marie apparently had enough one day and finally just beat the living shit out the woman. My mother, in telling me the story, also had a few Polaroid's of Vivian's face and I must say Marie had done a rather splendid job. Her face looked like a plum somebody had thrown out the car window at 70 mph. What comes around goes around. However, although my Mom had been granted custody, Marie was not living with her for reasons that were unclear to me. She was staying in the neighborhood and came to see me during my stay. She looked good. She was a woman. I was shocked! I had never seen her like that and it had been so long since I had seen her. Marie had really changed in appearance but her disposition was very much the same. Our visit was brief, 2 hours at the most and when it was time for her to go she gave me a big hug and made me promise to let her know if I was leaving so she could say goodbye before I left.

As you may imagine, there was a lot of anxiety in the air as to what the hell "Mark" was doing. Staying, going, what would I be doing with myself if I did decide to stay? Where would I be going if and when I left, the list goes on? Once again I had answers for none of these questions. Showing up out of the blue created a tension in the household and once again I found myself so preoccupied with trying to figure things out that I wasn't even giving my brother Chris the time of day. He would come running in from outside pleading, "Come on Mark let's go play some Frisbee, let's go for a bike ride!!!" Anything to get me to hang out with him, but I was a dud and always refused until one day my Mom had had enough of hearing me say no to Chris. She yelled at me, "what the hell is wrong with you that your brother has to beg you to play with him?" She was right, but I didn't know how to answer her. I hadn't givin' any thought to what kinds of pressure my being there and my not knowing "why" would impose on their everyday lives. My response to her at the time was nothing less than "FUCK YOU BITCH." We went to blows again, but this time I didn't run. When we broke apart from each other, I went straight to Chris's room to collect my things. Chris was there and he sat across from me as I collected my things. As I did, I just looked at him and said, "Why do you stay here?" To this day I have no idea what I meant by that. It's not like there was anywhere he could have gone. I

189

gave him a hug and said "I'll be back," and as I walked out the door I heard my Mom call out "Mark, be careful honey!"

Phewwwwwwww, ya know, I love my Mother and every time I saw her I missed her even more. I wanted desperately to have the kind of relationship that I had had with her as a child and I deeply resented the fact that it could never be like that again. We still had a great chemistry but the depth wasn't there.

I hit the first freeway onramp and, after getting stranded on an onramp in Watts for 6 hours in the burning 100-degree heat, I quickly discovered the difference between hitchhiking on the open highway and hitchhiking through the inner city of Los Angeles. I thought I was going to die in the heat and it didn't take long to realize I was in the wrong neighborhood. What with the fact that there wasn't another white person in sight and every black person that passed either pointed, gawked or gave me a mean stare, I could have allowed myself to get scared, but I didn't know exactly where I was and I knew that being afraid wasn't going to help my predicament. On one side of me were black people driving by...staring...and on the other side in the distance were skyscrapers with Chinese writing on all of them so yea...I was lost, but I didn't dare get off the on-ramp and walk into the city. Six hours later the one and only white guy to drive by picked me up and asked "What the hell are you doin' out there? Are ya trying to get yourself killed?" I was burnt, exhausted, dehydrated. I could barely get the words out "Studio City" and the guy said, "No problem."

32

Studio City is where Dorothy's parents lived. I needed a rest and I knew they would not only welcome me with open arms, but would also more than likely provide me with a bus ticket back to Idaho, and that's exactly what they did. Dorothy was, shall we say, less than impressed with me and the fact that I'd stolen her gun and disappeared. However, she was more *worried* than anything else and glad to see I was all right, but she was pissed about the gun. We avoided each other for weeks. I still shared a room with Rick and we were doing a lot of drinking together. I began to do a lot of partying with my brother Dan and a friend of his named Mike.

One night Mike showed up at the house with half gallon of Jack Daniels driving his Dad's brand new 1983 Toyota station wagon and wanted to party. Somebody came up with the idea of going to a place called the Roller Drome, a local skating rink. So off we go. We pick up a couple of cuties and we headed back to my house to finish off the whiskey. After about an hour of playing quarters and with over three quarters of the half-gallon gone, we were all slobbering drunk. At some point ole Mike and his cutie were laying back on my bed and its pretty obvious they want to use my room, so Mike throws me the keys and says, "Take a drive or something." So, I slide on my moon boots and head out the door with my cutie. Well, I don't know how but somehow I managed to drive around for a little while and somewhere along that two mile stretch of road that led to my house I decided I was gonna floor it. Have you ever tried to regain control of a stick shift at 80 mph while fishtailing during a blizzard after straight shooting a fifth of Jack Daniels with moon boots on? Don't!! The last thing I remember was taking my hands off of the steering wheel, looking over at my date and slurring out the words "Here we go", at which time she began to scream hysterically. When the car stopped, we were right side up in the dry irrigation ditch that ran parallel to the road. I was lucky that I came out of it with only bruises from the steering wheel on my legs, but even luckier that my date came out of it with only an egg sized bump on her head. We both got out of the car and proceeded up the hill to my house to tell Mike. When I walked into the room it was dark and I didn't bother turning the light on. I really didn't want to see his face when I told him the news. I just came right out with it "Dude...I just totaled your dads new car," he just laughed, "Come on dude, quit kiddin' around." I said, "dude, I'm not fuckin around, it's down there at the corner at the bottom of the hill totaled." He really didn't believe me until all four of us walked down, in the blizzard, and he saw for himself. And that's when he started crying and jumping around like a pogo stick. After a thousand, "I'm sorries" from me and twice as many "fuck dude", "what am I gonna do's", from Mike...we finally walked back up to my house and calmed down. After seeing poor Mike's reaction, my buzz was quickly replaced by the seriousness of the situation. I told Mike that I would take full responsibility, but I was shocked when he responded with, "are you fuckin crazy! If my dad finds out you were driving, "I'm" a fuckin dead man!" He went on to say, "dude, I've got to tell him I was driving" and he said he didn't want to hear another word about it and that's how it had to be. The next morning I found out just how lucky I was after they towed the vehicle. The police investigation revealed that based on the skid marks, the kind of damage done to the car and it's position, that it had begun to fishtail at approximately 80 mph, did two complete 360's and flipped 3 times end over end into the ditch. Mike said, "dude... you're lucky to be alive", and I thought to myself, "In more ways than one." Mike took the heat for the entire accident and man I was eternally grateful. Oh, his dad was pissed, but according to Mike it was nothing compared to how mad he would have been had he found out who had really been driving.

It was at about this time in my life when I had begun to enjoy the pleasure of singing with the band at parties and bars around Boise. I had a great many friends in both Nampa and Boise and it was at a party in Nampa where I would meet a kid named Jake R. Jake was a guitarist and, once again as a result of hearing me singing at a party, he was interested in knowing if I would be interested in singing for a band. I said "sure I would be happy to come check it out," but I had to let him know that I couldn't make any commitments due to the fact that I was already singing for a band in Boise. "No problem just come jam with us" he said, so I took down directions to their practice pad and showed up the next day. He introduced me to his brother Dan and the drummer Chris N. I remembered that I couldn't stay long because I had band practice in Boise, but it was long enough to EEK through a couple of Judas Priest songs. They were impressed with my vocal ability but honestly...they weren't the greatest musicians I had ever played with, but let me tell you something, they were some of the greatest personalities I had ever met up to that point in my life. These guys were just a hoot to be around. Jake's brother Dan, in particular, was a natural fuckin comedian. We hit it off right off the bat. It was one of those friendships where you're just constantly trading insults but there were never any hard feelings, although at times it was hard to tell. At the time, I was playing with a band called "Brighton." Bart B on drums, Andy D on guitar and Bob R on the bass. These guys were a heavy metal band. We did songs from bands like Iron Maiden, Saxxon, Judas Priest, and Ozzy Osbourne. They played loud and they played fast. Practice was at Bart's and it was always a party over there. We played a lot of parties, but nothing public.

One day I got a call from Dan R. He said we had a gig on some small island out in the middle of the Snake River. He never "asked" if I was interested, he just called to "tell" me we were playing and when. It's funny that for a guy like myself who doesn't like being told what he's gonna do, I was always amused by his pushiness. This was a great gig. It was on a privately owned Island and it was no holds barred fun. We played for so long without a break that I sang the last song laying on my back, unable to stand. The next party I played with Brighton, I had an argument with Bob and that was the end of that. It was only a matter of time because we never got along anyway.

Tony P was playing drums for a band called, "Tyrants Reign", a great bunch of guys. Dorothy had a tax seminar in Florida and said she was going to be out of town for about four days. That little light bulb above my head clicked on and above it the word "party" flickered. It was going to be a week or so before she left, so I had time to plan. We had a three-car garage that I thought would be perfect for a live band. I asked Tyrants Reign to play and the date was set. The first thing to do was clean the garage and set it up for a party. I took care of that and Dorothy was overjoyed thinking I had done it out of the kindness of my heart. About two days before the party I had a serious dilemma. I was *broke* with no money to buy the first keg. I hadn't the slightest idea how I was going to generate any cash to pay the band, but my brother Dan and good ole Mike came through. They said, "don't sweat it Randy, we'll take care of it" and on the day of the party they handed me enough cash for not only the first keg, but enough for the first three. The party was on and I was jumping for joy. This party was a hit to the tune of about 350 people, a little too successful, in fact. The first 3 kegs were gone in the first hour and we couldn't buy the booze fast enough. We ended up having to give some people the money back they had paid at the door because they were unable to get their cups filled. I was as apologetic as I could be because I really wanted everyone to have a good time, but with so many people that's the best I could do. All in all I think everyone had a pretty good time. I had a lot of close friends keeping an eye on things to make sure nothing was stolen and we all agreed that only the closest friends would be allowed inside the house. The police heard about our party, but all they did was wait down the street for people to leave. It lasted all night and Dorothy was due back that day and since we had no idea when she as going to be pulling into the driveway, we worked frantically cleaning up and getting rid of the evidence. This was not an easy task, but the cleanup went very smoothly and we were incredibly thorough, thanks to the help of a lot of very good friends. As a matter of fact, the place was a little too spiffy and that's what ultimately got us busted. Dorothy could tell something quite major had occurred at the house, but all she said was, "I know you guys are up to something, the place looks great...nothing is broken and nothing has been stolen, so there isn't much I can say." Whew, what a hoot!

You know, when I started writing this book, I had no idea in what degree of detail that I would be able to recollect the memories. So, as I sit here now... about to write more about myself, I can see why so much of that part of my life was so easy to recollect, it's because I hadn't seen nothin' yet.

33

In early 1985, I was 17 and coming off my second release from St. Anthony. Due to the fact that St. Anthony refused to release my academic records to Nampa High School, I found myself in the 11th grade with 8 credits. Needless to say, the idea of sticking it out in high school and graduating at 20 something was shall we say "unappealing", so I said, "fuck it" and quit. From that point on I did nothing but party and it drove Dorothy insane. She could rarely get a night's sleep with all the commotion coming from my room all night long. Doors slamming, music playing, cars coming in and out of the driveway... sometimes it was literally a zoo.

One night, Rick and I were having a little drink-a-thon with a half gallon of Seagram's 7. Well, we had a little disagreement and started throwin' blows. Dorothy came down and tried to break it up and by the end of the ruckus it somehow became "what the hell does Randy want to do"? I was still a couple of months away from being 18 and Dorothy decided she had had enough of me at the house because honestly, all I was doing was drinking and carrying on. It was time to do something and apparently she had given it some thought because she had a plan. She sat me down and said something to the effect of, look you seem to really enjoy your music, I would like to see you do something with it, it seems to be the only thing you enjoy doing anyway, so if you're interested, I would send you to music school. She gave me a choice between Berkley and Hollywood. To tell you the truth, I really wanted to go to Berkley, but as I had family in Los Angeles and if anything happened, I wanted to have somewhere to go. Also, Dorothy's parents lived in Studio City and I liked the idea of being close to them. The timing for this proposal was perfect from a musical standpoint because I had reached a dead end in my piano playing. I had taught myself as much as "I" could up to that point...but without the benefit of formal training, I was stuck. I could play entire songs but I had no idea what a chord was, nor did I know what a scale was. I didn't know the musical theory behind my compositions and, for that matter, I had never even heard the term "Music Theory". If someone were to ask me to play a C major chord I would have looked at them like they were crazy. For obvious reasons I decided on Hollywood. It's not clear to me how it was decided what particular school I would attend as there were several music schools to choose from in the Los Angeles area, but I think it's safe to assume that Dorothy had done her homework and had been able to narrow it down to the most professional and reputable school in the area. That school was "The Grove School of Music" in Studio City.

The location of this school was ideal since it was only about a mile or so from Grannies house. However, there was still the little matter of me auditioning and being accepted into the school...which little did I know meant that Dorothy and I would be sitting down with the founder of the school, Dick Grove and I would be asked to play a little something. It was shortly after I had turned 18, in 1986, that Dorothy and I flew down to Hollywood. We stayed at Grandma and Grandpa's and while I poured over literature about the school, Dorothy went out and busted her ass scouring the countryside looking for an apartment. It was agreed that we should not do this together basically because of the fact that there's a couple of things that you just didn't do with Randy. You don't shop for clothes and you certainly don't drive around in 100-degree heat looking at apartments all day in North Hollywood, even if it is for his benefit. I didn't care where I lived or what the place looked like, I just wanted to make the move to Hollywood and finally be left to my own devices. Dorothy was understandably leery about finding the place on her own without my being with her to see it, but I put it to her like this, "I know it's a lot of work and it's not at all that I just want to get out of that part of it, but you know as well as I do that you and I driving around in a hot car all day will only lead to a blow up of some kind". Dorothy agreed, but was still leery about my trusting her to decide on a place I would be okay with. I assured her that I trusted her judgment and that as long as she didn't mind doing it alone to "please" go ahead. I was still experiencing the shock of having this opportunity presented to me but at the same time I didn't want to seem lazy or so arrogant that I was above doing the work to make it possible. I just thought it would get accomplished a lot easier and sooner this way, and it did.

As excited as I was about moving to Hollywood, I did take the time to actually read some of the literature about the Grove School of Music. What I mean to say is that it could have said anything and I would have agreed to attend just to get out of Idaho, but the fact is as I read about the school I quickly discovered that this was going to be more than a matter of just being accepted...this was no school of slouches. A man who had written all of the music for Charlie's Angels, Jack Smalley, taught one composition class. A musician who played that music, Terry Janow, taught another sight-reading class and one of the choreography classes was taught by one of the street gang dancers from Westside Story, Bob Banas. These guys were long time-seasoned professionals in the music and television industry. We walked into Dick Grove's office and introduced ourselves. After expressing our interest in my attending the school, Dick explained the format and that there were only a couple of openings left open for enrollment and then he asked why I thought he should let me into his school. I was a little thrown by this because I hadn't really prepared myself. It was an unexpected question. At that moment it became clear to me that it wasn't just a matter of being approved for the loans it would take to pay for attendance, but there was also a question of talent. I quickly explained that I had been playing by ear since the age of 8. He had a piano in his office and said, "go ahead and play something". I could see by the photos on the wall of Dick Grove playing the piano that he was an accomplished pianist himself, and that made me a little more nervous, as if I wasn't already. It was way too late to turn back, so I pulled up the bench and very nervously muddled through my best self-taught progression. When I came to a stop he said, "Okay now play, Mary had a Little Lamb". I went to play "Mary had a Little Lamb" and bungled it miserably, however, I stopped and corrected myself. On each incorrect note I went back and played the right one without searching and that, my friends, is what got me into the Dick Grove School of Music. Had I not corrected myself, I would have been rejected.

Later the following week, Dorothy found a very nice and somewhat secluded studio apartment in North Hollywood. The agreement was that as long as I made a passing grade, my rent and utilities would be paid for the next year and I would be given $50 a week for food. If I felt like I needed more money I could get a part-time job, basically, I had it made. I began my first semester at the Grove School of Music, moved into the studio and was left to my own devices and "BAM"; I was 18 years old and living alone in Hollywood. Now, I'm a people person and that's all there is to it. I like to go out and just walk among the masses and what better place to do it than a city like Hollywood. (Besides New York "Smart Asses!") My apartment was quiet and secluded from the main street. It was hidden behind a house with many large and lofty trees. Very private! It was two story apartment with mine being upstairs and 1 of 6 individual units.

The night of my first stay in the apartment alone was a warm summer evening. I showered, dressed and had a couple of cocktails. I stood outside my door along the walkway at the railing and took it all in. There was a warm Santa Ana breeze blowing through the trees and I just stood there for a long while just listening to the sounds of the city: traffic; helicopters; sirens; the sound of jets going to and from Burbank airport; even the unmistakable sound of occasional gunfire in the distance. I took several deep breaths...I knew I was in love with this place. I had fallen in love with it a little more each time I would visit the Grandparents throughout my childhood years. I just loved the smell of the city...the unpredictability of it and I had always been infatuated with the pace and tempo of the city. Finally, here I was, smack dab in the middle of it...on my own...free to do what I want, when I want. It was exciting! I went back inside and took a couple of straight shots. I said to myself, "I'm going out tonight". I put on a light jacket, not so much for warmth but more for the purpose of concealing the large steak knife I planned on taking along with me. I had no intension of using it on anyone unless of-course I had to. I had never walked the streets alone, and though I had a pretty good sense of where not to go, I still wanted to be able to protect myself if it came down to it. I shut the lights off, turned off the TV and locked the door. I hit the sidewalk and headed for the corner of Burbank and Lankershim.

It was a busy Friday night and I waited at the pedestrian x-ing for that light to turn green before I crossed Lankershim. At that time there was a Denny's on the corner of Burbank and Lankershim and, from in front of the restaurant, I began to hear shouting over the traffic. When I looked up, I noticed a person standing on the other side of the street wobbling like one of those 4-foot blow up clowns with sand in the bottom. At about the same time I see another person take a running start and slam hard into the wobbling clown, sending him flying out into the street. I'll never forget the sound of his head hitting that concrete, like the sound of a ball pin hammer hitting a coconut. There was a break in the traffic so I took the opportunity to run across the street. It was pretty clear to me that the guy had had enough and as I reached him, the other guy went to start kicking him in the street. I shoved him back and said, "He's had enough!" The guy replied, "Oh…you want some too"? I began to reach for my knife and as I did so somebody (I'm assuming his friend) pulled him back, noticing I was reaching and said, "come on man you don't want none of that, let's get out of here". He took his friend's advice and they sped away. The guy was lying in the street in a pool of his own blood. He was a Hispanic man, extremely intoxicated, but still conscious. He could barely speak a word of English, but he knew how to say thank you for saving my life. He was crying and repeating, "Oh mucho gracious senor, you save my life, my family thank you, I thank you!" I pulled him out of the street just in time to avoid the next wave of traffic.

Once I had drug him onto the sidewalk, he begged me not to leave him and I assured him I would be right back. I could see he was losing a lot of blood as another pool formed around his head on the sidewalk. I ran into Denny's and told them to call an ambulance and then went back out to where he was lying on the sidewalk. I was amazed he was still conscious but there he was still thanking me. He kept trying to offer me money but I wouldn't take it. I guess I should have but it just didn't seem right to accept money from a man in that condition, which was ironic because when the paramedics arrived they scooped him onto a gurney and as they wheeled him into the back of the ambulance, his money began to fall from his front pockets into the street, only to be pocketed by the paramedics who simply smiled at me, shut the doors and sped away...siren wailing.

All this in the first block of my first night out in North Hollywood. I remember looking at the sky and saying, "what the fuck was that all about", before continuing on to the bus stop. Yes, I did think about just going back to the apartment, not because I wanted to chicken out about going out but because I needed another drink. Naaaa! I caught the bus to Hollywood Blvd. I wanted to see the stars on the sidewalk, the people, and the tourists. Everything I used to crave on my long walks and exploration adventures in Idaho was finally the inexhaustible source for my scrutiny and experimentation. I had an insatiable desire to see what it was all about. I would walk from one end of Hollywood Blvd. to the next. Going from one little trinket shop to the next, I stayed until late into the evening exploring the Blvd. I was mesmerized by all of the activity of the street. People everywhere, some of them dressed in the most ridiculous and outlandish attire you can imagine. One of the things I admired most about Hollywood Blvd was that nobody really seemed to give a shit about what anyone else thought about the way they were dressed. Even the way people went about their business was just that, their business. There were plenty of people selling drugs and I was approached numerous times. LSD, Pot…I would learn the hard way later that you didn't always get what you paid for when it came to an open street deal. I walked and explored until I became tired. I could have walked all night long but I had class in the morning. I had to tear myself away from it all. I again reminded myself that I had class in the morning and that none of it was going anywhere. I caught the bus home and passed out.

34

My first day of class at the Grove School of Music was mostly orientation. I decided to major in Classical Piano with a minor in vocals. My classes consisted of sight-reading, composition, choreography, stage band, ear training, and vocal training. Everyone was very friendly but considerably older than I. After the first week I was already very intimidated. In contrast with some of the other students, my talent seemed insignificant, but it wasn't only that, what really intimidated me the most was how dedicated the other students were. First of all, in addition to all being older, they seemed to know what they wanted to with the rest of their lives. I wanted to get along with everyone. I wanted desperately to at least appear as though I knew what I wanted and why I was there, but since neither was true, I found myself being uncomfortable for the most part. Most, if not all, of my teachers picked up on this as well as many of my fellow students. I'll never forget the first time I was asked to get up and sing in front of the class. A class full of singers...some very, very good singers and some very bad. Each pupil in the class was asked to sing in front of the class and then each classmate would critique you. It didn't matter what a person sang...it could be anything. When I got up to sing I chose something from a band called Rush. Back home, I had always been praised for having an ability to sound exactly like the lead singer from Rush. So I get up there and I belt out the first verse from one of my favorite Rush songs. Since I had always been praised for singing like that, needless to say, I thought I was pretty hot shit. When I stopped my teacher (a woman) looked at me from her chair (doing her very best not to laugh) and asked, "Who are you trying to sound like?" This was the last question I expected to hear and it was like a pile driver to the old EGO. The brutality of the question was that I instantly realized how ridiculous I must have sounded to a room full of people who wanted to hear "my" voice not my best mimic of someone else. The double whammy was having to admit to the fact that I was mimicking by saying who. I felt like an idiot and almost walked out but that would have looked worse so I endured the embarrassment. This was incredibly difficult for an 18-year-old spoiled brat with a temper he'd never had to control. In that one big gulp of pride I felt myself mature. I took my seat while the teacher explained to me the importance of developing my own voice, my own sound. She said that obviously I have a strong vocal ability with a great range but that she would like to hear "my" voice and that we would work on that. I sheepishly sat down but that day was one of the biggest blows to my ego that I had ever endured up to that point of my life. I never in a million years expected to be beat down with hard cold facts. I had never been in the company of somebody who knew what the hard cold facts were, but I never forgot where I was and I knew very well that there was much to learn from this person. Sometimes the pain is not in the knowing but in the growing. I told myself to sit down and shut up, and that's exactly what I did. There would be many times I would tell myself to sit down and shut up. Not only in class but also at home alone when it came time to study. I couldn't argue with the philosophy of the teachers at the Grove School of Music. It was simple. They would say, "it's your money and if you want to waste it and not learn anything by not studying, then go ahead." It was no sweat off their ass. I was already uncomfortable; I didn't want to look stupid too. Though I still couldn't keep up, I studied as much and as best as I could. One of the hardest classes to study for was sight-reading. I would spend hours writing notes on the staff. Treble and bass clef, and then timing signatures and note value, scales, the circle of 4ths, the circle of 5ths, major, minor, augmented and diminished chords, inversions of those chords. It was enough to make your head spin but I knew that this information (music theory) was vital to my becoming a better pianist. This was something I knew I would have to learn if I wanted to continue singing my own music and there was no getting out of that for me. So I studied. I also dove head first into learning every technique I knew I would need to know in order to develop my own singing style. One day I stayed after class and explained to my vocal instructor that I had sang for a lot of garage bands, some of them heavy metal, back in Boise. I went on to explain that there were many times when I had experienced excruciating migraine headaches during practices and performances. She asked me to describe them. I said the pain isn't constant but actually only occurs when I stop singing and that's when it hits me like a freight train. Sometimes it's so bad I almost pass out. She said, "I notice you like to sing high, ya know just cuz you "can" doesn't mean you "should" and certainly not all of the time. Now do me a favor, take a big deep breath for me." I did so and when I exhaled she said, "Did you notice how when you did that consciously your stomach went inward." I said, "yea...so?" When we take air into our lungs our diaphragm expands outward, not inward, but it takes practice. Once you train yourself to breath properly and strengthen the muscles in your diaphragm, you can then begin to take some of the strain off of your vocal chords and divert it to the much stronger diaphragm. She went on to explain that by straining for those high notes all of the time I was creating a constriction around the smaller blood vessels in my neck while straining. Once I stop straining, the blood begins to flow and BAM! Hello Migraine! She showed me some of the proper breathing exercises and I spent the next month doing them in my apartment over and over and over.

I was still spending my weekends on Hollywood Blvd. and it was on one of those excursions where I would stumble onto a couple of old friends from Boise. It was a hot Friday night and as usual I happen to be Bee-Bop'n along Hollywood Blvd just going about my business checking out the freak show when I came to the corner of Wilcox and Hollywood. I stood there at the crosswalk and lit a cigarette trying to decide if I wanted to continue up Hollywood Blvd or turn right on Wilcox. I decided on Hollywood even though

I had been up and down probably 10 times already that night. I was enjoying the show. It was unusually busy and when it's like that you never see the same thing twice. I walked about half way up the block and, don't ask me how, but somehow in the midst of all of the people and commotion and car stereos blaring, I managed to hear the sound of a very familiar laugh as I passed by the doorway of one of the many paraphernalia/T-shirt shops. Upon hearing it I stopped dead in my tracks and entered the store. As I made my way toward the rear of the store my suspicions were indeed confirmed. There standing with their backs to me were two friends of mine from Boise, Idaho. Dave and Gary! Dave had been the bass player for Tyrants Reign and Gary was a guitarist who had been Dave's roommate and a friend to both of us through the years. I snuck up behind them and didn't say anything, just waiting for them to turn around. The last time I had seen Dave was at the party at my house in Nampa where, several times during the party, he would take me aside, refuse to take no for an answer, and hand me his pint of Tequila saying, "drink." Man, I hated that stuff but I liked Dave well enough to let him talk me into drinking it down every time. We had developed (Dave and I) a greater camaraderie every time we had seen each other during those early years so it was all hugs and handshakes when he turned around and saw me standing there. Dave said his apartment was two blocks up the street on Cherokee so the 3 of us decided to go there for a beer. This was truly a dream come true for me because, not only did I now

211

have friends to hang out with but it also meant I had a place near the freak show (Hollywood Blvd) to hang out at. And hang out together we did, from that point on we were inseparable.

35

Apparently, Dave's parents had sent him to Hollywood also to attend music school. The name of his school being MIT or The Musicians Institute of Technology. The apartment complex where Dave and Gary were living was filled with musicians attending MIT, thus opening the door to an entire circle of new friends. I remember most of their names, Larry, Joe, Doug, Ron and some characters whose names I can't recall. The summer of 1986 in Hollywood was hot and crazy. We partied our asses off and soon became known to many if not all of the street people along the tourist area of Hollywood Blvd. There were plenty of them to be known to as well as shop owners and restaurant owners. There were also a few runaways that we took into Dave's apartment, however, that was short lived after we discovered things disappearing around the place. We never asked for anything from them or tried to impose our will and we were pretty pissed to find our good nature being taken for a ride, so that was the end of that. I loved hanging out at Dave's, but I had the best of both worlds in the seclusion of my apartment whenever I wanted to get away from it all, which incidentally wasn't very often.

Dave's place was a security apartment meaning you had to be buzzed in. There were a couple of times I went there and no one was home to buzz me in. One hot night, in particular, I stood outside smoking a cigarette, waiting for someone to come home or buzz me in when, very quietly, a gray station wagon with tinted windows pulled up in front of the complex across the street. I casually watched as they opened the back of the station wagon and retrieved a gurney. I could see on the side of the station wagon the circular California State Seal along with the words Los Angeles County Coroner, so it was obvious what they had come for...and sure enough about 20 minutes later here they came strollin' down the steps with a body all bagged up nice and neat. They opened the back, collapsed the wheels, slid it back and left just as quietly as they had arrived. I remember flippin' my cigarette onto the sidewalk and saying to myself, "nice neighborhood" as I turned and walked down Cherokee toward the Blvd.

I spent some time getting to know my own neighborhood and my neighbors. The neighbor to my immediate right was an interesting character. His name was Bob Z and he looked like a plump version of Radar O'Riley from "MASH." I met him one night while hanging out on the walkway outside my front door. He had just returned from the store and was carrying his usual 24-pack of Milwaukee's best. We said, "hello" and introduced ourselves to one another. Bob invited me in for a beer. I remember his apartment looked like a throwback from 1969......in fact, I think Bob had lived there since then, and he only came out to get that 24-pack and or a bite to eat when necessary. I'm talkin' hard-core recluse. The night I stepped into Bob's apartment was like stepping into a time machine. We began to drink and listen to the Doors and Frank Zappa. Bob was literally stuck in that era. Besides drinking beer, Bob's other preoccupations were guns and sports statistics. This guy was an absolute sports statistic phenomenon. He could tell you the stats on any player from any sport old or new. I liked Bob well enough and we talked late into the evening and at one point I got up to get us both a beer. Our apartments are identical except that I noticed his kitchen window has a screen. It's a metal screen and I notice there is a small hole in the lower right corner of it, not thinking anything of it, I casually make mention, "well at least you've got a screen on your window, mine doesn't have one, but did ya know ya have a hole in it?" He says, "Yea... a couple years back I was drinkin' with a buddy of mine when I ran to the store for more beer and I came back to find him with his brains blown out all over my kitchen." That hole in the screen there is from the bullet ricocheting off his skull. As if it weren't weird enough, he went on to describe how the cops had simply removed the body and left him to wipe up the brain matter. Yea, good ole Bob the neighbor guy. Needless to say I tried to avoid being his drinkin' buddy in the future...but we always got along just fine.

As my schooling progressed there began to be more interaction with fellow students in some classes. For example one of my composition classes required us to be paired with another member of the class and we were asked to do a cold read, something from a script provided by the teacher except it wasn't really cold as we were allowed to rehearse at home with our partner during the week before class. My partner was a girl named Christa N. We had decided that first rehearsal to be at my place and yea, we rehearsed...a little and then we had sex! Well, what can I say, she wanted it, I wanted it, it just happened. I began seeing Christa but I didn't want anything serious. I was only 18 and Christa was somewhat older, besides, I ended up meeting the girl of my dreams a couple of months afterwards.

36

The girl's name was "freebase", "freebase cocaine" and I, like so many other unfortunate souls of the 1980's, fell head over heals in love with her. We were first introduced during a visit with my sister Marie and her then boyfriend, Steve...in San Pedro, CA. To this day, I still remember the taste. We smoked it using a cotton ball on the end of a hanger dipped in Bacardi 151 and the first real good hit I got wound me up like a doll with a string comin' out of his neck. I just couldn't shut the hell up. I kept goin' on about how awesome I felt and about every other sentence was, "hey, let me try that again." Yea, the rush from freebase Cocaine only lasts about 5 minutes, if you're lucky, and then you spend the rest of the time trying to recapture the initial rush. Sexy little drug but really just a flirtatious tease. However, its seduction is so powerful and metaphysical that its addiction is instantaneous. I wish I could find words to describe the feeling but I've been sitting here for the past hour trying to find them and the only ones I can come up with are "there are none."

I was a couple of months into school when Grandma and Grandpa bought me a little Riva Scooter to get back and forth from school. I went everywhere on this thing. I mean everywhere. I began making trips from Hollywood to San Pedro to see Marie and Steve (Marie's boyfriend) at Steve's house. I would take the $50 a week I got for groceries and have Steve walk down to what they called "The Lows" and buy freebase Cocaine

(Crack). The "Lows" were project style Navy barracks that had been converted for civilian occupancy but still patrolled by shore patrol. Militarized Federal Law Enforcement. It was a ghetto but it was Steve's neighborhood, which meant it was safe for him to buy dope off the street. This is something I had never done and if I had tried I would no doubt have been ripped off, beat up or worse, but I did go with him on numerous occasions. One of the first things I noticed was that once we walked into a certain part of a neighborhood everyone knew what we were there for. It's like it was the only thing we were allowed to be there for because if you were down there just walking about------you might have a problem. Everyone knew Steve and I did my best to take that into account. There are rules to an open street deal. The first and perhaps most important rule is to never pull out a wad of money. Have only the amount required for your intended purchase, ready and in hand. Never make any sudden movements, like reaching for an inside jacket pocket. An armed street pusher is likely to misunderstand or misinterpret your body language and you could wind up shot. Never give your money to someone who says, "we'll be right back", because they won't and if you do---- you've just been robbed. Always taste the rock. I've bought salt rock, wax, sheetrock, peanuts and all because I didn't taste it before I handed over the money. What you look for in the taste is the numbing of your tongue and a bitter medicinal taste and sometimes even this can be faked. However, by tasting it at least you can be sure it's not

218

wax. Never let yourself be pressured or rushed. For example, "Come on, Come on!…Give me the money, hurry up!" FUCK THAT! Make it quick but make sure you know what you've got before you hand over the money. I could go on forever about the do's and don'ts of an open street deal, but no matter how experienced you are there is always a chance you might get ripped off. The ways to rip a person off out number the ways to prevent it. The fact is that most all open deals are commonly conducted in the worst neighborhoods of a city and you can bet that it's always a dangerous undertaking.

After making the buy we'd make our way back to Steve's house and the 3 of us would lock ourselves in their room away from Steve's Mom, who always quietly watched TV and never bothered us. Marie would take out a box that contained a glass pipe, a broken piece of hanger with a cotton ball on the end, a pint of Bacardi 151 and a wad of "Char Boy" brillo to be used as a screen for the pipe. She would quickly take the bottle of 151, unscrew the lid and fill it with rum, placing it on the dresser. Steve would take out the dope…and start breaking it into little pieces. Marie would wad up a small piece of brillo and burn off all of the shininess with a lighter. She said, "because it's toxic" (as if the dope isn't, but hey, why rush things)…she would stuff it in one end of the pipe, drop a couple of pieces of cocaine on the screen, dip the cotton ball into the cap of 151, light it with the lighter and begin a nice and slow steady draw. We all took our turns at this until all of the cocaine was gone and then we would all be good and high. I would sit on the edge of the bed yapping away until the sound of my voice became an annoyance to everyone including myself. Marie would usually pop off with a quick, "shhhh", whenever Steve's Mom would walk by outside the bedroom door on her way to the bathroom. The high from smoking freebase cocaine is so all consuming and powerful that the slightest increment of coming down is an insane impact that is simultaneously replaced with a desperate craving for another hit like you've never felt in your life, but wait...that's not all!...if you call now you'll also get this complimentary "CLUCKERS" kit! That's right folks, at no extra charge you to can spend hours "clucking" like a chicken, picking at the carpet for any white crumb that even remotely resembles that kibble of coke that you know dam well you didn't drop. These mysterious crumbs and kibbles can include, ramen noodles, popcorn, plaster and if you're lucky you might even pop a bugger in that pipe and smoke it! Hey, anything for another hit. When it was all smoked up we would all try and force ourselves to sleep, laying there, listening to the sounds of the neighborhood...with one thing on all of our minds--------more dope! The come down from freebase cocaine, with the exception of lost love, is the most uncomfortable experience I have ever known. Unfortunately, the sensation of the high is so addictive that the consequence of how horrible you feel when it's gone is seemingly irrelevant at the time. But, like it or not, when it is gone you're faced with an inescapable desperate craving for more. So desperate in fact that many who become addicted to freebase cocaine eventually lose all of their personal possessions to the drug...and this includes ethics, morals, integrity, and any self esteem that may have existed prior to when it all began...and from the moment it all began for me, after the first hit off that freebase pipe, it all "began" to become more of a blur...slowly at first.

For one thing, in order to support this new obsession I knew I was going to need more money. At the time, my friend Dave was delivering pizza for Domino's on La Cienega in W. Hollywood. Dave had mentioned that he was sure he could get me a job taking phone orders and making pizza at night. I filled out an application and was called in for an interview. The store manager was a young Asian kid by the name of Sim. Sim sort of resembled Mr. Sulu from Star Trek. He was an extremely easygoing character and we hit it off. I got the job and Sim asked if I could start that night. I agreed but asked him if I could go home and change first. He said, "no problem." So I hopped on my little Riva Moped and sped up La Cienega to Sunset Strip. It was a Friday night so the traffic was heavy with cruisers and streetwalkers. Oh yea, lots of prostitutes. Well, I got about as far as Sunset and LaBrea, right about where Ralph's Supermarket is and I guess I must have had my eyes on something or someone other than the road because at about that geographic location I heard the screeching tires of the Cadillac in front of me and slammed chin first into his

221

trunk…screeeeach…BAM! The next thing I knew I was lying on the sidewalk clutching my balls gasping for air, looking up at a punk rocker with a pierced nose and a pink MOHAWK complete with gothic style makeup. He was quite casual in saying, "dude…your chin is gashed wide open, we're having a little party, but you're welcome to use my phone." It was a little while before I was able to respond since at the point of impact the steering bar had bent back into my crotch. I was unable to speak or stand and I was totally oblivious to the gash in my chin. In the meantime the old fart I hit was nice enough to come over and make sure I was all right and handed me his card. All I could do was nod at the time. I finally regained my composure and was helped up by "Mohawk Man" and in a real cool and casual manner asked, "Care for a cocktail?" I said, "Fuck yeah!" He said, "let's hit it man." I'll never forget that guy. Can you picture Tom Petty with a Mohawk and a nose ring? Well, that's the dude. Anyway, I went to his place and used the phone. The only person I could call in such an emergency was Grandpa Jack. He's the only one I knew with a truck. It was a while before he got there because of traffic, but that was fine because the drinks kept comin' and Tom Petty (Mohawk Man) assured me I was welcome to hang out for as long as I wanted. I called my new boss, Sim, and explained what had happened, which was a little difficult with all the music and party commotion in the background, but surprisingly, Sim was very understanding and said, "just come in tomorrow." Gramps arrived on the scene along with Grannies brother Uncle Sam and by that time I wasn't feeling any pain. We loaded up the moped in the truck and headed to Cedars Sinai Hospital for a couple of chin stitches. When it was all said and done, Grandpa and Uncle Sam dropped me and my smashed moped off back at my place. I thanked them a thousand times and apologized for having to call. The bike was smashed but still rideable so I was still able to get to school and start work at Domino's the next night.

I liked this job and it wasn't long before I became quite good at it. You might be thinking,"nothing to it, phone orders and making pizza"...but actually there is something to it, for one thing you have to be fast at making pizza and not everyone can do this. And for another thing, you've got to be good at taking orders over the phone from people who don't always know what they want...but there's something else.........you see, West Hollywood is the gay capital of Los Angeles so most of the orders I was taking were from "flamers"...ya know...fags, queers, homosexuals, cross dressers, he she's...whatever have ya, no not me----you. Anyway, I'm a guy who's always looking for a way to put a little comedy in the job, just enough to take some of the monotony out of an 8 or 10 hour shift. Now a lot of these phone orders I had comin' in were from fags who were, to say the least, very flirtatious and at first, I was a little taken back and uncomfortable with this...but then it hit me, hey, I'm not delivering these pizza's...Dave is...so I began to flirt back. Almost every time I did this, the caller would ask, "will you be delivering", and I would answer, "as a matter of fact I will, my name is Dave and I'll see you in 30 minutes or less." Then I just had to make sure that Dave took that particular order. I would always watch his facial expression and demeanor upon his return from those deliveries. Sometimes he'd be pissed, sometimes happy as a clam, but I never told him what I was doing, even to this day. Had I told him what would I have had to laugh about all those nights?

When we weren't working at Domino's, we both could be found walking up and down Hollywood Blvd talking to various street people and eating at weird restaurants. Sometimes we would go to Sunset Strip and hit the clubs: The Roxy, The Rainbow, Gazzarri's and sometimes even the Troubadour on Santa Monica Blvd. One night Dave and Gary said they knew about a band named 'Snair' that they wanted to hear play at the Troubadour, so we all went. These guys were from Detroit and they played original music. My best description of their music (to coin a descriptive title), "Motor City Heavy Metal." These guys were kinda creepy but they were cool. Every hair on their bodies was dyed jet black and they all had shiny black fingernails. After the show they invited the three of us to a little after hours party where they were staying. They gave us directions and it was easy enough to find but none of us had ever been that far down Hollywood Blvd before and we were in for a rude awakening. Ya see, if you're headed down Hollywood Blvd and you get a little past Vine from that point on the neighborhood gets a little less friendly with each city block. In fact by the time you reach Hollywood and Garfield, you're in the ghetto...at least this was the case in the year 1986. The night we were invited to party with "Snair", we were (me, Gary and Dave) all on acid and by the time we made it to this never before seen dirty end of Hollywood Blvd we were at the peak of our high. Now take three guys from Boise Idaho, give them some LSD and drop them off in a nasty neighborhood and what I mean by nasty neighborhood is this...picture yourself being approached, or maybe mobbed is a better word, by people of just about every ethnic background offering just about every illegal drug you could think of. The Mexicans were offering "Pot", the Blacks were offering Crack, the Cubans were selling Heroin and at the same time all of this is going on there are transsexuals, he-she's and hookers, hanging out the windows and on the fire escapes of the "Snair" apartment building trying to lure us in by flashing their nasty unnaturally hormonal grown breasts and saying in voices much too masculine, obscenities of the most vile context imaginable. To the street pushers we would say, "no thanks, I'm cool, I'm good", but this only works for so long because, just like Steve's neighborhood, you have to have business in a neighborhood like this to be there. You can't just wander around because if you linger, pretty soon you're gonna have a problem. We went up to the front desk and apparently we were early because Snair hadn't made it back from the club yet. After an about face, we walked out of the large building onto the sidewalk. All three of us were pretty high by this time and for a short while we were all just dazed and mesmerized by all of the weirdness going on around us. It was Dave and I who first felt a little tension coming from a couple of the pimps who were watching their girls…and then a couple of street pushers abruptly brushed by me in passing. We both looked at each other and said, "let's get outta here." We started to make our way back down Hollywood Blvd with Gary trailing behind. We could hear him saying, "hey where you guys going", "what the fuck?" Not far behind Gary, Dave and I both notice a little Hispanic dude wearing a long trench coat and walking with a slight gimp. He's coming up pretty fast and Dave and I are lookin' at each other with this, what's-wrong-with-this-picture-look, on our faces. Well, I'll tell you what's wrong with this picture: first of all it's 80 degrees and this guy is much too small to be coming up on us with the mad dog look he's got on his face. Any one of us could have whooped up on him…but this guy is fearless and relentless in his pursuit. In the meantime Gary is still back there saying things like, "what the fuck", totally oblivious to the situation. Dave and I, in an effort to get this guy off our ass, cross the street and the guy doesn't follow. He stays on the other side and reluctantly Gary finally crosses to our side. Once we reach the freeway overpass the guy slows down, does an about face and heads back toward Garfield. We'll never really know what the little guy's intentions were but, if you ask me, you don't have to be a genius to see that we had stumbled into the wrong neighborhood. We weren't buyin' dope, we weren't looking for a date and we didn't look like cops...so quite simply we were viewed as a threat and escorted out of the neighborhood. I would bet my life on it and I guess you could say I did. Any Joe Blow reading this book might say to himself "paranoid", but any street person will tell you that the scenario I've just described is neither far-fetched nor paranoid.

After we made it back to Dave's, and while Gary spent the rest of the evening playing his guitar to a band called "Septic Death", Dave and I decided we weren't high enough so we ate some more LSD. We had a bunch of it. Somebody on the Blvd was selling it in bulk. It was a blotter style LSD called "Blue Note". One quarter the size of a postage stamp with a picture of a blue musical quarter note on one side. We spent the rest of the night walking, laughing, singing, talking, laughing, laughing, and laughing. We drove to Venice Beach just as the fog was rolling in from the ocean and from the lifeguard tower we watched what I could only describe as ghosts in the mist performing a romantic ballet. Without looking away from it I said to Dave, "Are you seeing what I'm seeing?" He said, "yeah" and in stereo we both said, "damn good acid"...funny.

Dave and I ate a lot of Blue Note LSD that summer and we shared a lot of bizarre and sometimes-hilarious experiences. I'll never forget the two of us passing a store front and looking over to see an obese woman in a full clown suit holding balloons saying, "Hi...I'm Giggles." We both saw her at the same time and couldn't stop laughing for two blocks. I think what made it so damned funny was that it wasn't a hallucination and when your high on LSD everything seems so staged that it seems specifically designed for your entertainment and there in lies the humor…but sometimes that specification is a long way from funny.

After seeing Giggles the clown, we stepped off of Hollywood Blvd and started up Dave's street (Cherokee). At the time, there was a restaurant called Love's Char-Broiled Restaurant and directly behind it was a parking lot bordered in by a four-foot cinder block wall. We came off of the Blvd still holding our bellies, and gasping for air as a result of the giggles sighting. We were laughing so hard we had to stop and catch our breath at the cinder block wall. Once we finally stopped laughing, we noticed it was completely quiet. There was a lull in the street traffic as well as the foot traffic. It's interesting the way that works on Hollywood Blvd in that early on in the evening all traffic is constant, but as it gets later and people start to go home, there becomes long moments of silence between waves of traffic. From the moment we stopped laughing and sat down on that cinder block wall an unusually long silence and break in the traffic began. It was a very warm evening, at about 2am and it was still about 78 degrees. Once we had stopped laughing and had just begun to regain our composure, a strange ice-cold breeze seemed to blow right thru us giving us both goose bumps. Dave looked over at me and said, "whoa", that was weird"…I had just managed to respond with, "you felt that too?"...when we both noticed a large group of people (about 50) come off of Hollywood Blvd up Cherokee heading in our direction. In the lead was a street kid we were both familiar with named Nicki. Nicki was known for taking in runaways and pimping them out, a real piece of shit. The crowd was about half street people we knew and the other half appeared to be tourists we'd never seen before. They all walked right on by where we were sitting on the wall and into the empty parking lot behind "Love's." Then they made a big circle as Nicki proceeded to kick the living shit out of some unfortunate tourist. The timing was weird because as soon as the fight began, so did all of the surrounding traffic. It only lasted as long as the next lull and then, as suddenly as they arrived, they were gone...another arctic chill blew through us and it was again dead silence with just the two of us sitting on the wall. I remember turning to each other and saying simultaneously.............. "Now that was fucking weird!" We both agreed that if we ever told anyone the story, that nobody would believe us...but a large part of the pleasure in writing this book is dedicated to the fact that contrary to what people "believe", I know what I lived---------because "I" lived it...and still am!

37

There were times when Dave and I just wanted to get high without having to mess around with the pressures of an open street deal and there are many...many jive assed...fast talkin' puff heads out there who know all too well how to talk a weary street beatin' white boy out of his cash. Some of these guys have just the right disarming delivery when it comes to the catch phrase, "I'll be right back." I don't care how street wise you are it's gonna happen. You give 'em your money, they walk away with a wink, a sudden look in the eye and their best reassuring smile and that's the last you see of them. The thing is you know it's gonna happen when you hand them the money but sometimes you're either too high to conduct yourself in a transaction or you just want to believe the dude is for real...and that's just what we were doing when we went rollin' down Hudson Street with our last $40 dollars..."lookin"...at 3am. We were rollin' by one of the many well-known Hollywood puff houses in a neighborhood where if you roll down the street, slow enough, inevitably someone will approach the vehicle and ask what ya need. A guy approaches, talks us out of our $40 bucks, says he'll be right back and we park a short distance up the street to wait-----and wait-----and wait. Now, the puff house the guy walks into is one of those run down weekly motels where you have to know someone who lives there to be buzzed in. After about an hour of repeating, "this is bullshit", back and forth to one another, I finally decide times up! I'm going in after this guy. Now, as we approach this place I'm immediately taken back a bit by the desk clerk who appears to be an androgynous transsexual with whom something terribly wrong occurred during the operation, never mind the size 12 shoe and the male theramone. As we walk in and approach the front desk, the first thing out of its mouth is, "that guy ripped you off, didn't he?" I answered, "Yeah, you want to buzz us through so we can recover our money?" (S)he says, "I can't do that but if you give me about 5 minutes I guarantee I'll get your money back and bring it out to you because I don't want see anybody get ripped off." (S)he sounded genuinely concerned for our $40 bucks, even indignant about the idea that the guy thought he could take our money and then hide out in "it's" motel...so we agree to this...turning to face each other with a cursory look that says "fair enough." We return to the vehicle to wait the 5 minutes. Not three minutes into the wait, slowly and creepily, with headlights off, an LAPD squad car pulls up and stops in front of the motel. The two officers step out and proceed into the motel to have a little chat with the androgynous Herman Munster. Right about now Dave's got his hand on the ignition keys but I insist, "NO." I say, "look we've been drinking and if we leave now they'll only follow us or radio ahead for us to be stopped up the street." I say, "Here's what happened. We were driving by and noticed an altercation between a man and the desk clerk so we stopped to check it out and that's why we're sitting here. That's our story." I was barely able to get our story straight when I noticed the officers exiting the motel and start to approach our vehicle, one on each side. "Go ahead and step out of the vehicle for us gentleman", the two LAPD officers commanded Dave and I. As we do we're asked what do we think we're doing. We offer the altercation story and with a stone cold unconvinced glare the cop in charge looks me straight in the eye and says, "I don't think so! I think what's happened here is that you gentlemen gave your money to someone with the intention of purchasing narcotics, you got ripped off and you think if you hang out long enough you'll be able to catch the dude coming out. Now I suggest you both get your little Idaho (license plate) Candy Asses back into your vehicle and drive the fuck away from here and, if we see you or your vehicle in this area again, you can bet your little candy asses you'll be going to jail." As we drove away there was a long silence between Dave and I until I finally broke the silence with the announcement of my theory on what had just occurred. It seemed to involuntarily escape from my lips. I launched into it, "so the puff head gets our money and when we're not so quick to leave 'Herman Munster' calls the pigs for back up, or protection, which has probably already been paid for through a weekly installment. The puff house gets our money, the pigs run us off slowing down the traffic, which keeps the voters happy and it's business as usual on Hudson St." The experience of that single incident offered an insight into the big picture that I don't think either one of us had ever even considered or fathomed before. The word "humbling" comes to mind.

By the time we both began to see the big picture, our lives were already seemingly out of our own control. It's a strange brand of oxy moron to witness your own life spinning out of control. You could stop it, but you don't. You just watch like a bystander, whose involvement is anything but innocent, but still only subconscious and inadvertent. I can't speak for Dave, but for me it was more than the drug, it was the city, the danger, and the act of putting my ass on the line every time I wanted to get high. That in itself was an addiction...and it was an addiction that would remain in my life for many years to come.

Our friend Gary managed to make it out of Hollywood without having to live through crack addiction. The whole scene just didn't agree with him. One day he said he was driving to Irvine Meadows for a big concert. It was a 3-day event and we became a little concerned when he hadn't made it back by day 7. We later learned that he had decided to just not come back. Instead he returned to Idaho, never to return.

Shortly after Gary's departure, Dave met a girl named Natalie. Natalie was a dancer, yeah, a stripper. She moved in with Dave and the 3 of us got along quite well...for a while we just partied our asses off. Dave's place was always littered with bottles, cans and overflowing ashtrays from the previous nights party. I suspect this kind of activity was largely responsible for what led our friend Gary to make his decision to flee. After all, we were all supposed to be there attending music school, ya know-----studying, but it was a constant ongoing party for Dave and I. So much so that even Natalie started to become unnerved, which was understandable since they never had any time to themselves as a result of my never going home. They began having quarrels about the way Randy always just comes in and helps himself to whatever he wants...he never goes home and just makes a mess. Dave would say, "We all make a mess!" Natalie would say, "yeah, but we live here." Through most of the arguments I would be sitting on the couch waiting for them to emerge from the bedroom so I could open the fridge and ask Dave why there wasn't anything to drink. Yes, I antagonized her unmercifully and pretty soon there became a competition for Dave's attention. I won. I think what did it was the way Dave would laugh right in front of her and the way I would just blatantly antagonize and get her goat. It all started as a joke that all three of us would laugh about together...but since Dave never drew the line, I never worried about where it started or stopped, so pretty soon Natalie decided enough was enough. Somebody always goes too far and in this case it was definitely me. When she left Dave he was visibly hurt and I don't blame him because Natalie was cool. I felt bad when she was gone and I could feel a hint of animosity from Dave towards me, but Dave could never say "no" to me and, not only did I know this but, I took advantage of it. It was all in fun and I never really meant any harm. I certainly wasn't out to wreak his relationship with Natalie; I just wanted someone to share the experience with. The "experience"...that's an interesting way to put it. Really what I wanted was Dave (no, not that way). Dave and I had a unique friendship. We seemed to have many of the same interests and the same appetite for destruction. When you find a friend like that in the middle of exploration in a city like Hollywood, it's impossible to imagine any other companion. A companion who is just as unfamiliar with the environment and is taking it all in...in such a similar tempo and view is hard to come by. The exact chronological order of events escapes me, but in the last days of my stay in Hollywood our companionship dissolved. We grew apart. Eventually Dave lost his apartment and moved in with me, but that didn't last.

38

I wish I had a penny for every experience I've had where words weren't enough to describe it...but words will have to do won't they? As anyone can imagine it was quite difficult to effectively attend school and keep a passing grade while taking LSD, smoking cocaine and hanging out on Hollywood Blvd. Somehow I was able to pass the first semester but my performances were weak because I was so nervous. It was obvious to my instructors that I had a preoccupation. I would show up late, wanted to leave early and my level of participation was minimal. I knew that they were there to teach me, not motivate me or baby-sit me. I became terribly overwhelmed and seduced by the vices of Hollywood and Los Angeles, completely subdued by culture shock and my preoccupation with the cocaine only became worse.

My experience in Hollywood can best be described as a stormy evolutionary graduation from the tiny microcosmic perception of what I believed to be *reality* (up to that point in my life) to the immense and brutally honest macrocosm of social awareness I had so ruthlessly thrust myself into. Out of the many things I learned about myself (in the city), the one that surprised me the most and stood out in my mind the most, was my appetite for self-destruction. Maybe it evolved through the dangers of so many bizarre open street deals.

Sometimes Dave would accompany me to see Marie and Steve in San Pedro. It meant more money and that we could buy more...but I learned very quickly that when you're smoking freebase cocaine more money means nothing because it's never enough and more people only makes it uncomfortable. Nobody really wants to share and so when it's all gone everyone is just sort of left standing there glaring at each other with an accusing look that says---------fucker! My addiction escalated at an incredible pace and pretty soon I had no intension of sharing with anyone. I wanted to take my rock to my house and smoke it all by my greedy little addicted self. By the time I was ready to start buying my own dope off the street, any fears I may have had about an open street deal were buried underneath by an incredible need for the drug. There was only one place I knew of that would accommodate my need...the corner of Garfield and Hollywood. It took about a month of getting ripped off and acquainting myself with the rules of the game...and after a while I only had a few people I would buy from...but that never stopped the unknowns from approaching.

One night I was approached by a couple of black dudes. The one doing all of the talking and wearing a vinyl trench coat and smoking a Virginia slim, walked up and unfurled a hand that looked more like it belonged to the crypt keeper from "Tales from the Crypt" and said in the most scratchy jive assed voice I had ever heard, "Hey...motha fucka, I got the mobile bouillon!" I got the double ups!" So I reached into his creepy hand and tasted one of his rocks. It was wax...and I threw it back into his hand and began to walk away. I think I only made it about 3 steps before this guy steps in front of me and starts chesting me with his little chickin' chest, saying in that scratchy jive assed voice, "heyyyy, mutha fucka! you owe me twenty dollas!...you bit off my rock!" His big assed buddy was behind him and his vocabulary consisted of one word, that obviously he had spent hours yelling into a mirror with a lot of bass, that word being, "YEA!!!" Well, my tendency to pay close attention to the rules of the game was to my benefit. Had I not done so I could not have possibly known that one of those rules was that selling fake dope on a street where real dope can be found is a violation of street law. Its simple, selling fake dope is bad for business and can ultimately ruin things for all of the real pushers in the neighborhood. So I merely chested him back and replied quite loudly, "watch'yall doin' down here sellin' BUNK DOPE!?" With the emphasis on "BUNK DOPE", instantly these two were surrounded and being pushed around by a group of some of the more legitimate businessmen in the neighborhood (for lack of a better phrase). As soon as that happened, I broke from the crowd and went on my way down the sidewalk, only to be approached by someone selling the real thing, thirty seconds later. "Wheeewww", so much for the Black Crypt Keeper and his sidekick BoBo.

Both Dave and I quit our jobs at Dominos on La Cienega but soon found ourselves working once again side by side at another pizza place called 7777 Sunset Strip. Dave got me the job there and, after about one week of employment, I exploded in the kitchen throwing a tantrum that resulted in my immediate dismissal. I remember that day well, not only because it was my 19th birthday, but because later that day I had to face both Dorothy and Dave back at my apartment. That meant I had to provide Dave with an explanation for my tantrum and Dorothy an explanation for what the hell was going on with school, my attitude, and me. The pressure was tremendous, especially when you consider the fact that I had answers for none of those questions. I had it made, but I was pissing it all off. I felt guilty because I really didn't feel I had any right to feel pressured but, worst of all, the only thing I could think about was getting high. All I wanted to do was escape and that's exactly what I did all the way up until the time came for me to move back to Idaho. Dorothy had no intention of continuing to pay my rent if I wasn't going to attend classes and I didn't blame her. Dave's father bought him a truck and after filling it with all of his stuff he disappeared from my life, but certainly not forever.

It was probably about that time when I really began to wonder if I was going to make it out of Hollywood alive. I began to realize that I-was-driven-by-the-drug and yet I was helpless against it. The anxiety fueled feelings of anticipation just before an open street deal. It began in the pit of your stomach and then surged to your head, most of the time leaving you sweaty and almost breathless and, depending on where you would go to buy, often times the anticipation of getting high combined with the possibility of impending danger would result in a sickening feeling of imminent implosion. There is really only one word for a drug that can make you feel all of those things and yet still drive you to doing it, "*evil!*" I'm inclined to ask, "What drug isn't?" There are plenty that aren't and as for those that are, I would definitely put freebase Cocaine at the top of the list of most "*evil*" drugs to become addicted to. There were plenty of times when I couldn't stand to wait the time it took for the bus to arrive at the stop and take me home before I had to have a hit; sometimes hiding behind the nearest dumpster to hit the pipe and even a few times hitting it as I walked straight down Hollywood Blvd., right in front of God and everyone. I didn't care who saw me. There came a time when the only thing that mattered was getting high and so I threw myself head first into it dismissing any and all dangers. In fact, I even robbed a couple of crack dealers myself but soon found out, after being recognized and getting the living shit beat out of me, that robbing the dealers only minimized the number of places I could go to cop. It didn't matter to me that I could have been killed or worse, the only thing that mattered was that I might run out of places to buy dope.

For the first time in my very young and inexperienced life, I began to feel like I was loosing sight of who I thought I was and, since I was too young to know who that might be, it was impossible for me to gage the loss of whatever control I had so foolishly convinced myself into believing I had.

But "I" wasn't the only one I had convinced. I had also convinced Dorothy, to some degree, that I could handle school, LA and myself. Apparently, I had convinced her to a degree far beyond what I was realistically able to deliver. They call it, "biting off more than you can chew." I mean, here she was putting me through music school, paying for my apartment, giving me the opportunity of a life-time and look what I was doing to show my appreciation...pissing all over myself and her good nature, but the last thing I was going to do was call her up and say, "Uh---hey, just thought I would call, say I love ya, and let ya know I'm hooked on Crack Cocaine".........I don't think so! But ya know something, it wasn't even the telling her about my new drug problem that made me not pick up the phone, it was more the idea that I had failed...not only in my eyes but in her eyes and my Grandparent's eyes. It might as well have been the eyes of the world, not to mention the eyes of God. All the shame in the world could not have prevented me from the one thing that pissed me off the most...the fact that I was *afraid* to call home. Sure, I was ashamed and didn't want to be an embarrassment to Dorothy or a disappointment to my Grandparents, but even with all of those considerations weighing heavy, a caring and understanding voice to speak to would have really, really been a nice consolation.

It was a very, very confusing time in my life. I could feel my own identity slipping away from me and I felt completely defenseless against it. I have done my best to illustrate what I believe to have been the circumstances of the environment in a number of scenarios that I feel are most accurately responsible for my personal evolution into the personality I am today. Since it is so incredibly difficult to grasp the mood of my perception throughout the vast multitude of evolutionary experiences in a 20 year span of time, it has proved to be an interesting as well as therapeutic process of re-acquainting myself with not only who I believe myself to have been, but also who I believe myself to have become as a result of who I once was. I am not a psychologist and I have never received any psychiatric instruction or training, therefore it should be noted that my own psychological observations are no doubt biased, hypothetical as well as purely theoretical all throughout. It is also important to note that certain characters included in this book may undoubtedly have differing opinions with regards to who Randy Snowball was at certain stages of his life.

I feel that in order for those family and friends, who have an interest in this book, to have a clear conception of my mind at age 20, it is necessary to discuss exactly what kind of relationship I had with God at that time of my life. I am not a "religious" person by the traditional definition of the term, but by the age of 20 I had just begun to figure out that spiritual growth in it's earliest stages is a journey of knowledge and not faith, and that in order to escape the preconceptions of our previous experiences and free ourselves of transferences, it is necessary that we learn.

I wanted desperately at this time in my life, more than ever, to increase my conception of knowledge, however I lacked the articulation and experience that would have been required to incorporate all of the information to a self-sufficient degree of organization. Very slowly and very gradually what I began to discover is that as I grew in life and love and discipline, then too did my understanding of the world and my place in it grew, but for every profound discovery there was always this neatly packaged option to self-destruct or recklessly trample and disregard the progress. That self-destruct option is what ultimately led to failure to grow in my worldviews and understanding. I think that for most of us the image we come to perceive of ourselves is a manufactured one provided by our peers and validated throughout school years. I believe we all want to be liked as opposed to being shunned, so it's much easier to fall in step with the image "they've" provided than to attempt to convince the majority that the image "they've" provided is incorrect. Doing that would mean going against popular belief and then showing everyone who you really are...and who knows who they really are at that age? Nobody! We think we do but we don't. Most of us want a kind of peace without the aloneness of power and the self-confidence of adulthood without ever having to grow up. A personal realization didn't even approach my comprehension for many years, but a little voice gave birth in my subconscious and began hammering it's way into my conscious mind very early on. However, like so many of us, I had this huge vision of a spiritual evolutionary process for myself, yet I undoubtedly lacked the will or even the stomach for it. I actually believed it was possible to skip over the discipline and find an easy shortcut...and had convinced myself into believing I could do so simply by imitating the superficialities of my idols. Imagine that, to think I actually went around imitating the people I looked up to. What an absolutely NORMAL thing for me to do. We're all raised on influences, desperately in search of an identity, but who we become is in direct relation to how well we know ourselves and that's a process that can't be rushed no matter how introspective we are. My experience (as I believe to have been that of all of us as human beings) has been a somewhat painful journey. Along the way I have been challenged daily to re-examine my old mind set with a simultaneous peripheral subconscious knowledge that relentlessly encourages my spiritual evolution through suggestions to my conscious mind. Exactly what pieces of the old mind sets should be discarded, updated and incorporated into the new and ever changing ones are some of these challenges.

This is where in life we must decide to either remain comfortable or endure the pain of growth. Since very few of us are willing to accept the idea that something so painstakingly constructed as a mindset or way of life could ever need to be updated or require replacement, most choose to remain comfortable...but the fact remains that all of us, at some point in our lives, will become restless for ways to explore new frontiers and enter new arenas. I believe that by nature we are all born with a built in curiosity about our own spiritual evolution...and there can be no doubt that opportunities to do so are made available to us all the way up until the day we die. Unfortunately, very few people are willing to do the often exhaustive and intimidating work that is required for the perpetual process of spiritual evolution. That having been said, we may be inclined to ask, "why?" If we are all extended this equal opportunity (through the grace of God) to experience this wonderful process of self-extension called spiritual evolution, why do so few of us choose the path? Perhaps because in the backs of all of our minds we know that along that with becoming more spiritually evolved comes an increased and complicated responsibility to share the knowledge...the well roundedness so to speak, and considering what it takes to get there. It's hard to imagine sharing it...let alone acquiring it.

Strangely, as hard as it may be to imagine, the desire to do so still exists. It would seem that the more spiritually evolved we become, the more eager we are for others to know and share the peace of mind. This doesn't come without its frustrations. Not everyone is interested in peace of mind and my idea of it probably bears no resemblance to the next guy's version, but when all of this "coming-about" is happening it's hard to get away from tunnel vision.

I came back to Idaho with the impression that many of the people in Idaho who had never known anything more than a mountain for a skyline were selling themselves short and, to this day, I still believe that anyone living in a small town owes it if not to themselves, then at least to their children, to see a city skyline filled with skyscrapers. Small towns are great to grow up in, but there is a lot more going on out there and, if only for the sake of awareness, I strongly recommend getting a glimpse of it. I believe that if a kid grows up into adulthood without ever seeing the Los Angeles City skyline on his way through Orange County to Disneyland then his parents have done him a great disservice. I suffered no such disservice in coming of age. Not only had I seen the ominous city skyline of skyscrapers but I had also been a part of the evils within it.

Upon my return from Los Angeles I quickly became known in circles, old and new alike, as a personality that could be counted on for seeing things for what they were and telling it like it is...subtle at first but no less brutally honest. I was no longer Randy Snowball, the singer who would try to sing anything even if it killed him, NO...I was now Randy Snowball, the singer who knew his vocal limitations and didn't mind saying so, but I wasn't an asshole...yet! This must be the part where the differing opinion of who I was comes in. I'm sure Dorothy would beg to differ on who I was upon my return. We were at odds and that is putting it mildly. She was disappointed in me and so was I. Her opinion of me mattered to me a lot more than I would have admitted at the time...but I resented her disappointment in me because, as far as I was concerned, she was acting as though the entire experience was a fiasco, as if I had come away from it with nothing. Although I knew in my heart that she really was hoping I would find success in my musical endeavors, at times I couldn't help but wonder if her disappointments weren't based strictly on a combination of the social embarrassment and monetary cost I had caused her. In any case, I knew I had learned an incredible amount about music theory and vocal training exercises but Dorothy never bothered to ask what I had learned academically, no...she was just disappointed and her behavior reflected it, so I ignored her in every conceivable way. I was disgusted with myself for seeming to be incapable of completing my schooling. I mean, after all...I had always been told how intelligent and talented I was, but I was also disgusted with Dorothy for being more disappointed than interested in what I had learned.

Something had really gone dry in the rapport between Dorothy and I since the days when we used to cry together and, even then, she had never been one to confide in. I was once offered a record contract by a shady production company and after sitting for 4 hours talking to Jim D and David S, I went home and woke her up to ask what she thought I should do. After describing the circumstances of the situation I could barely get her to roll over and say, "do what you think is best." And advice about the birds and the bees...these subjects were never broached and no voluntary attempts were ever made by Dorothy to discuss these issues, at least not with me. I can't speak for the others but I do think it's safe to say that we would all agree Dorothy is not the easiest person to approach. I sincerely hope she can appreciate these criticisms every bit as much as she has appreciated the credit I've given her in this book. I would like very much for those who read this book to grow along with me as I grow by writing about my personal experiences in life...hence the title, "The Snowball Effect." Fortunately for the reader, the author is the only one who can truly experience the conclusion of a book like this.

I had no conception of the degree of life long commitment Dorothy had pledged to me and I was paralyzed by my fear of commitment. I had no idea how to deal with what was happening between Dorothy and I. I wanted to talk with her about my experience in Hollywood, but she seemed indifferent toward me and I was angry with that. I have always wanted a relationship based more on a friendship context than the maternal one that always seemed to get in the way of my willingness to relax and open up to her. I felt like her interests were based more on my responsibility to her as a son, as opposed to my responsibility to myself (as a person) to do something with myself. It was always upsetting to me to consider what we had been through together, and yet for some reason we were still unable to be friends, one of the many prices I would pay for a defiant disposition. I just didn't trust anyone who said they loved me and unfortunately for me, I still don't. I've chosen poorly in those I wanted to trust and ignored the people I should have trusted, which made it that much harder to trust my own judgment to choose wisely. What a way to live, sometimes (early on in life) it's not always as "cut and dried" or as simple as a matter of choice.

Choices can be complicated by the circumstances of an environment, but only early on. Obviously this doesn't apply to adulthood where we become solely responsible for recognizing the circumstances of a bad environment, but I'm getting off-track here. My own complications with trust, not only with the people who wanted desperately to love me (Dorothy) but also with myself, obviously stemmed from the lack of a stable environment and what I came to believe was the "abandonment" by my natural mother, Becky.

It was ten years before I ever saw her face again (between ages 5 & 15) and, during that time, I was left to draw my own conclusions about what happened to her. My conclusion was "abandonment"...and no one ever disputed it. By the time we were reunited and I finally did hear her side, quite frankly her explanation wasn't good enough. She tried to explain that on that day in 1972 she had been arrested for a probation violation and jailed. She believed someone would come home, find Marie and me and would know to take us to Grannies. She went on to explain that her incarceration had lasted a year and that all during that time she did everything she could to find the two of us, but to no avail. The authorities were completely uncooperative and there was nothing she could do to regain custody or even locate us. I'm afraid that after 10 years of wondering, crying, hating, blaming, losing the ability to be close to my sister, clenching my fists in rage and staring up at the sky cursing God, there wasn't anything she could have said to make me forgive and forget.

Although I had managed, by the grace of God and through the care and patient therapy I had received in St. Anthony with Barbara F, to discard the bulk of the volatile violence of my anger, I'm afraid Barbara and I were not afforded the many years it would have taken to bulldoze the layer upon layer of defense mechanisms I had constructed.

There's a lot to it, this thing we call trust...and once it's lost the process to reclaim it is painstaking at best. Through out the years my reluctance to trust has cost me many, many friendships and relationships that I deeply regretted losing after they were gone. However, by the same token as a result of my choosing poorly, trusting has also been costly. I say "as a result of my choosing poorly" as if it were a casual realization, but quite the contrary, in fact it should be noted that it was literally years before I evolved beyond "poor me", "nobody loves me", and blaming God for the decisions I was solely responsible for making. In fact, for years I was convinced that every negative outcome of my poor choosing only solidified my poor self-esteem and proved that God was out to get me. But God wasn't out to get me.....I was.

END OF BOOK 1

Biography

The author was born in 1967 in Los Angeles County, California. His parents separated and divorced when he was young leaving him living with his mother, sister, and his mother's extended family. Unfortunate circumstances led to his separation, along with his older sister, from his mother at age five and the beginning of several foster case placements. Eventually adopted by a family at age eight, he acquired three new siblings and struggled to become part of a disintegrating family. Within a year this family relocated to Idaho, his new parents also divorced, and a single, working mother raised him.

Unanswered questions about his birth mother and the circumstances of his abandonment, coupled by frustration, molded him into a very angry child, teenager, and young man. Problems with authority have plagued him all his life. The book covers the first twenty years of his life, to the best of his recollection.

The next twenty years found him pursing his musical career, living in Los Angeles, working in Las Vegas, acting as a caretaker in Boise, Idaho for his adopted maternal Grandmother during the last years of her life, in and out of jail mostly for DWP (driving without privileges) offenses, and continuing his struggles with alcohol and drugs.

At present the author is an inmate in the Idaho State Prison system serving a seven-year sentence for probation violation. Realizing his inability to live under the rules of the probation system, he is determined to finish his entire sentence, without early release, in order to be free of the probation regulations and restrictions. Randy married in 2006 and his wife is patiently waiting for his release.

Made in the USA
San Bernardino, CA
06 December 2017